YOUR CLIENT'S STORY

KNOW YOUR CLIENTS AND THE REST WILL FOLLOW

Scott West and Mitch Anthony

Dearborn™
Trade Publishing
A **Kaplan Professional** Company

President, Dearborn Publishing: Roy Lipner
Vice President and Publisher: Cynthia A. Zigmund
Acquisitions Editor: Mary B. Good
Senior Project Editor: Trey Thoelcke
Interior Design: Lucy Jenkins
Cover Design: Scott Rattray, Rattray Design
Typesetting: the dotted i

Published by Dearborn Trade Publishing
A Kaplan Professional Company

Printed in the United States of America

05 06 07   10 9 8 7 6 5 4 3 2 1

Library of Congress Cataloging-in-Publication Data

West, Scott, 1959-
    Your client's story : know your clients and the rest will follow / Scott West and Mitch Anthony.
        p.   cm.
    Includes index.
    ISBN 0-7931-9570-5
    1. Financial planners.   2. Investment advisors.   3. Customer relations.
    4. Interpersonal communication.   I. Anthony, Mitch.   II. Title.
HG179.5.W47 2005
332.6′2—dc22

                                                                    2005004959

C ontents

THE END OF THE PROCESS AS WE KNOW IT

"When we become attached to our models or our roles, we impede the discovery process that our clients need. Ideally, we need to surrender to the conversation and allow something far richer to occur than could be contained in any model or professional orientation."

Courtney Pullen, Ph.D.

Dealing with money is not like dealing with any other product or service in the world—and it is high time to stop treating money like it is. Money is a deeply personal and deeply emotional issue. We are just now beginning to understand the deep and transcendent meanings of money in our lives. Financial philosopher and director of the Integral Finance Center, Richard B. Wagner, offers a brief but incisive definition: "Money is an agreement on how we exchange the best we have to offer. Money is the most powerful and pervasive secular force on the planet." And, quite often money is an agreement of the most sacred sort. "I am trading what has been paid for with my heart and strength for a promise you are making in return." What price was paid to gather this money? This is where we begin to discover the meaning of money.

There is a multigenerational dramatic story linked to each individual's money—stories of hard work, sacrifice, risks taken, miserable failure, and fortuitous breaks. There are stories of fortunes lost and fortunes found and obstacles overcome. There are other stories of traitors and benefactors, adversity, and peril. Each personal money story has its roots in the lives of our antecedents and the price they paid to help us gain a footing in this life and continue on through our lives to our heirs and the shining hopes and ambitions we carry for their betterment. These dramatic stories continue on through them and the generations and dreams they spawn.

The story of money in our lives would be better told by an Alex Haley than it would by a reporter for the *Wall Street Journal.* Yet many people in the money business continue to treat the topic of money as if it was merely a product or service to be sold with processes that don't fit with the nature of money. You can't just take a selling system used by Procter and Gamble to sell soap and apply it to someone's life savings. Money goes much deeper than that. You simply cannot do justice to people and their money with approaches based on "fact finders" and "selling opportunities." People feel that they are nothing more than a collection of facts or a mark for a monthly sales quota. They want you to understand the depth of the meaning of their money.

Money is not comparable to other goods and services that are traded. What product or service carries this level of emotional impact? Buying a car or a house is an emotional event but doesn't compare to turning over the trust regarding the fruit of toils over a lifetime. Hiring a lawyer or some other professional to help manage a life event is one matter but hiring a professional whose reach will impact the quality of my life ongoing is quite another. Sales processes that have their origins in selling boxes of soap and tubes of toothpaste will hardly suffice here.

The time has come to address the client relationship at a higher level—not as a sales opportunity, but as a connection with a life story in progress. Your roles will include biographer and financial director. Don't settle for the low ground of selling props. At the end of it all, you know you have helped your clients if you have played a role in helping their "stories" end well.

Recently to a graduating rookie class of the best and brightest advisors, we posed the question, "What is money?" You would assume that if individuals were planning on making a living in financial services by helping people manage their money lives, they would have a lucid definition and articulate thought around the raw substance of their trade, which is money. But these learned students sat slack-jawed at the question. Finally someone ventured, "It is a representation of value." Another offered, "It's a material symbol of value and worth." These abstract definitions continued until one student, in an attempt to cut through the nebulous fog, stated, "Money means something different to every individual," to which we replied, "Indeed it does." We then asked, "How can you succeed in this business without knowing what that 'something different' is?" You certainly won't discover the unique and individual definition of your client's money while you are busy fact-finding and categorizing, ultimately force-fitting your clients into a predetermined product or service. If facts, numbers, and products are the only services you are able to provide, then it's time to look beyond your process.

We believe that coming to the end of the process (as we know it) will mark the beginning of real curiosity in our practices.

GOOD BIOGRAPHERS FEEL NO NEED TO DOMINATE A CONVERSATION

Many financial conversations are based on control: the control of the provider to dominate the conversation, lead the witness, and/or draw foregone conclusions. An entirely different approach based on genuine curiosity is fueled by a desire to know—simply for its own sake—which in turn evolves into empathy and manifests itself in the form of real and vital solutions. Controlling questions backfire. Like the barricades they put up on highways under construction—designed to control your movements but emotionally cause you stress and the desire to exit as soon as possible—conversation controls lead to adverse emotional reactions.

Is it possible that the need to control is based on fear? Fear of not having the right answers, fear of not appearing knowledgeable in front of the client, and fear of being wrong. This fear is based on an outdated metaphor that the client is the pupil and the advisor is the teacher who must have all the answers. The new metaphor is that of coaching or collaborating with clients. Exercise genuine curiosity and release yourself from the shackles of fear. What do you have to fear as a biographer? Only that you failed to get the whole story.

This new conversation, which is focused intently on discovering the client's story and facilitated by the skilled biographer, will be the hallmark of success in financial services in the years to come. Clients' money will flow in the direction of the provider who, motivated by curiosity, discovers their heart and soul in the stories they tell.

A study commissioned by VanKampen Funds, and carried out by Prince and Associates, demonstrates the economics of our assertion that money flows in the direction of biographical knowledge.

The study looked at 319 affluent investors with investable assets ranging from $600,000 to $1.2 million. The average assets per investor were $801,000, and the average number of investment advisors (IAs) was 1.76.

All the investors rated the extent to which their IAs knew the answers to a battery of questions. That is, the affluent investors determined if they believed their IAs knew certain information about them. The accuracy of these assessments was never determined.

Using a variety of statistical techniques, 22 key areas of client knowledge were identified from a list of 148 questions. Furthermore, eight core areas of client knowledge were identified. The degree to which an affluent investor believed each IA knew these key areas is a predictor of the percentage of the investor's wallet an IA had.

The affluent investors were statistically divided into three groups:

Group One

- 77 affluent investors (24.1 percent of the sample)
- Only one IA
- Average investable assets: $834,000
- Number of referrals in the past 12 months: 4.1
- Believed their IA could correctly answer 18 to 22 of the key areas of client knowledge
- Believed their IA could correctly answer seven or eight of the core areas of knowledge of the client's life.

Group Two

- 141 affluent investors (44.2 percent of the sample)
- Two IAs
- Average investable assets: $769,000
- Number of referrals in the past 12 months: 1.5
- Believed their IA could correctly answer 12 to 19 of the key areas.
- Believed their IA could correctly answer four to eight of the core areas.

Group Three

- 101 affluent investors (31.7 percent of the sample)
- Two IAs
- Average investable assets: $819,000
- Number of referrals in the past 12 months: 0.1
- Believed their IA could correctly answer 11 to 17 of the key areas
- Believed their IA could correctly answer three to six of the core areas.

When an affluent investor employs more than one IA, there is a difference in the quality of the relationships between the investor and each IA. When an affluent investor detects genuine curiosity in the advisor, the need for more than one advisor evaporates.

The study examined groups 2 and 3 with respect to each IA the affluent investor was using. One IA had the majority of the client's assets—the primary IA. The other IA was referred to as the secondary IA.

Group 2 (141 Affluent Investors)

Description	Primary IA	Secondary IA
Percentage of Group	70.2%	29.8%
Average Investable Assets	$571,000	$198,000
Percentage of Client's Assets	74.2%	25.8%
Number of Referrals	1.9	0.7
Number of Questions	14–19	12–16
Number of Core Questions	6–8	4–7

Group 3 (101 Affluent Investors)

Description	Primary IA	Secondary IA
Percentage of Group	51.5%	48.5%
Average Investable Assets	$476,000	$343,000
Percentage of Client's Assets	58.1%	41.9%
Number of Referrals	0.2	0
Number of Questions	12–16	10–16
Number of Core Questions	3–6	3–6

The bottom line is apparent. The more you know about your clients' lives, the more insight you will have into the financial story woven into their lives, and the more trust they will be willing to extend in regard to their assets. You will find the core areas of inquiry in this book revealed in their proper context—curiosity, not manipulation. Or, as one veteran advisor stated: "For 17 years I've talked to people about their money and just hoped it was connected to their lives. Now I talk to them about their lives and help them understand the connection to their money."

It's not a story of numbers that you need but a number of stories. Your client's financial life is but one thread woven into the fabric of his or her total life. The more genuine curiosity you exercise, the more evident the pattern in that fabric becomes.

Your client's story reveals his or her purpose. Your business success hinges on how closely aligned you are with that purpose. We hope that this text will kindle the flames of your curiosity, ignite empathy in your client relationships, and bring a sense of life and excitement to your business like you have never before experienced.

1

THE MAGNETIC POWER
OF CURIOSITY

"I have no special talents, I am only passionately curious."

Albert Einstein

"The desire to know is natural to good men."

Leonardo da Vinci

Fanatical Curiosity Keys

1. Your interest level in others is the emotional foundation for succeeding with others.
2. Many selling approaches pay only lip service to inquiry and consequently raise the defenses of the client.

It was the second year in a row that Mitch was delivering a keynote speech for a company's President's Club banquet. When the awards were handed out, he noticed that John Sigmund had finished number one, as he had done the year before. He also noted that the distance between number one and number two for both years was similar to the distance between first place and second place at the 2000 U.S. Open, when Tiger Woods beat Ernie Els by 13 strokes. John had again lapped the field.

Mitch asked someone if John did this every year, to which he replied, "Every year that I can remember."

This aroused Mitch's interest in learning what made this advisor tick. He approached John after the banquet and asked if he would be willing to have dinner with him the next evening and John agreed. Mitch told him he was going to give him a homework assignment before they met again. He asked John to try and distill the key to his advisory success into one word.

"OK," John said. "I'll give it a try."

The next evening John informed Mitch that he had found the answer to the question, and it had only taken him 45 seconds! He told Mitch, "I can't thank you enough for asking. It forced me to think about why others are attracted to me and my business."

The word John offered was a description of his nature. If we were to pause here and allow you, the reader, to try and guess the word, chances are you would not get it on your first ten guesses. (We have performed such an exercise in sales training sessions and John's key word doesn't come up in the first 30 guesses.) The word he gave was *curiosity*.

John explained it this way, "I thought of all the words others attribute to sales success—hard work, goal-oriented, people skills—but decided that the one feature people take notice of about me is that I am naturally a very curious person. I love learning about people. They all have unique stories to tell, unique paths that they have taken, and unique hopes for the future. I like hearing about my clients and their children and grandchildren. I think clients like this about me, and so they tell their friends about me."

Curiosity may kill cats but for people, the abundance of curiosity gives life to relationships, according to research conducted by Todd Kashdan, Paul Rose, and Frank Fincham at the University of Buffalo. Ninety volunteer subjects completed two Curiosity Exploration Inventories (CEI) developed by the researchers. The subjects were randomly assigned as conversation couples. These 45 couples were then introduced to two experimental situations: One designed to generate interpersonal intimacy and the other to mimic a small-talk situation. Each couple spent a total of 45 minutes talking and asking specifically designed questions in a predetermined order.

The results were as follows:

- Those with high CEI scores directed more attention to their relational partners, capitalized on positive features of their personal interactions, self-generated interest and fun by being playful, were responsive to their partners' interests, and contributed novel ideas and topics to the conversation.
- Subjects with high CEI scores reported feeling significantly closer to their partners, and their partners reported feeling significantly closer to them, than did subjects with low CEI scores.
- Considering that their interaction was only 45 minutes long, the extent of the closeness generated between the high-curiosity individuals and their partners was surprising. They all reported feelings of closeness above the conceptual midpoint, even when comparing their feelings to other relationships in their life.
- During the potentially dull and boring small-talk encounters, those with high CEI scores reported using their wit and further questions to liven up the conversations, thereby transforming them into much more interesting dialogues.

Researcher Kashdan commented that, "Individuals with high levels of curiosity exhibited approach and pleasure-seeking behaviors irrespective of their social context that increased the likelihood of positive social interpersonal outcomes such as shared feelings of intimacy between strangers."

The implications of this study on the financial services business and its attendant conversations are enormous. Amazingly, subjects in this study reported feeling "closer" to someone they had just met through a 45-minute conversation than they did with people whom they had known for years because of the superficial nature and lack of curiosity in those relationships.

This dispels the myth that it takes too much time to really get to know your clients. False. *It's not about the amount of time spent; it's about your curiosity level and the quality of your questions, which are the two topics that we will address at length in this book.* Advisors like John Sigmund figured out this emotional fact early—and now, success as an advisor is as easy as a good conversation.

"ENOUGH OF ME TALKING ABOUT ME . . ."

John's compelling success is due to a curious nature, which holds at bay his own inner rumblings for attention, glory, and credit. These self-indulgent inner rumblings, which show through in conversation and behavior, are what we refer to as the *narcissistic urge.* Our favorite example of this urge is the guy in Hollywood who said to his friend, "Enough of me talking about me, how about you talk about me for a while?" Overinflated egos and personal insecurities are just two of the forces at work contributing to the obsessive tendency to pull every conversation into orbit around ourselves. Ultimately, the narcissistic urge provides emotional discomfort for others who will either avoid the narcissist or stop taking him seriously.

How prevalent is the urge? To answer the question, first ask yourself about the last time you were in a conversation where the person you were talking to could not ask enough about you. Do you remember such a conversation? Of course you do—if such a conversation ever took place. Some people have told us that they have had only one or two conversations like that in their lives! The lesson learned is that selflessness is in short supply. This is strikingly obvious at any cocktail party. Controversial qualities not in short supply are: one-upmanship, egotism, megalomania, self-promotion, and what we call the "Clark Kent" conversation pattern in which stories are designed to make one look like Superman.

Make mental notes in your next ten conversations regarding the polarity of these conversations. Are the other persons trying to create a polarity around you or themselves? Are they trying to create equal polarities? By observing these polarity patterns you will feel admiration for some people, disgust for others, and pity for many. Most importantly, you will move to a higher level of awareness about the polarities you are creating with your conversation patterns. Beyond the aesthetic "How are you?" greeting, the majority of people you meet either don't know how to or don't care to make further inquiry. A clear—but negative—example of this lack of "others" focus is the jaded (and narcissistic) salesman who said, "I'll tell you the people I can't handle. The ones who when you ask, 'How are you doing?' think you actually *want* to hear the answer!" Obviously this individual's sales career has not been anchored in empathy.

HOW DOES IT MAKE YOU FEEL?

What is the emotional impact on clients of a narcissistic approach? Again, ask yourself how you felt the last time you were engaged in a conversation with a monopolist? In our advisor training sessions we often ask this question, "How does it make you feel when you are trapped in a conversation with a person who dominates the conversation?" One participant quickly replied, "Married." On the serious side, the answers we often hear are: "bored," "angry," "frustrated," and "unimportant." When you peel away all the layers of the emotional onion, this is the visceral impact of conversational monopolists—making themselves appear important.

Self-centeredness and self-absorption are common to all humans to varying degrees. Narcissism—the endemic cancer of the human psyche and personal relationships—severs the ties of commonality and connection. It is the condition of mind that prevents the development of empathy.

The narcissistic mindset causes us to look at another human through a reflecting lens, thereby limiting our vision. Instead of looking at another person and seeing a window through which we can perceive who they are and what is important to them, the narcissist can only see a mirror. Narcissists can only think of who they are and what is important to them. Genuine curiosity, however, radically transforms the chemistry—not only of the situation but of the brains of the participants as well.

Modern psychology reports that curiosity creates a biological reaction called the "interest/excitement continuum" (identified by Dr. Sylan Tomkins), which reveals that the more interest I demonstrate for you the more exciting the conversation becomes for you and the more interested you are in me. Chemicals are released in the brain that fuel this cycle and the result is a connective psychological phenomenon we call empathy.

Psychologist David Morrison of Morrison and Associates in Palatine, Illinois, describes it this way: "From the biological point of view, psychologists have learned that studying 'big cats' like cheetahs is more advantageous than studying apes because the defining characteristic of the big cats is curiosity, which is intrinsically linked to survival and pleasure. Curiosity causes you to go out into your environment to find new things; a new mate, new food sources, new settings."

"I'm not going to get my clients interested and excited in me if I'm not interested and excited about them. Just being interested in and curious about your clients is going to make them interested in you. As soon as you break that cycle of interest and excitement (like with a manipulation to make a sale), the chemistry falls apart, shame enters, and all the good done to this point is diffused."

There are some professionals who do not have good inquiry skills because they are simply not interested in others. But there are also many others who do not have good inquiry skills because they simply have not been taught how to make a meaningful inquiry.

We think we can offer help to both.

For those who do not think they are interested in anyone else's story, we invite them to take the "empathy challenge." Empathy is something we experience when we take the time to hear someone else's story and put ourselves in that person's shoes. Individuals who say they are not interested in taking the time to hear their clients' stories invariably have family members and friends whom they empathize with because they know *their* story. That is why there is a meaningful connection. We dare anyone to ask some of the questions posed in Part II of this book and observe the empathetic connections that form as they listen to the profound stories that their clients have to tell.

Many individuals have never been taught any sort of inquiry other than the one designed to benefit themselves and their companies. Many of these individuals would like to evolve into a discovery process that is indeed discovery. Either they've never discovered the mutual satisfaction of a conversation powered by curiosity or they simply lack a path to empathy or a protocol that is sufficient for client discovery. The Financial Life Planning Model of Discovery, introduced in Chapter 6, "Merging the Quantitative and the Qualitative," will provide such a path.

THE SIGN AROUND EVERY PERSON'S NECK

Years ago, a sales veteran told Mitch to observe a young, exuberant sales professional and try to figure out if this new sales professional would get the sale. Mitch admitted that he didn't know if the young man would make the sale or not. This sales veteran said, "I can assure you that he will not get the sale. If you carefully watch his conversation you will observe that he has not yet figured out who matters most in this conversation. He thinks it's about him and his product." He went on to say, "Always remember this one important fact: every person you meet is wearing a sign around his or her neck that very few people know how to read. The sign has only four words on it, but 95 percent of those competing for the business don't have a clue as to what it says. The four words are *'Help me feel important.'*"

We don't believe that we can pass on any more important instruction than those words. Everyone wears that sign, and so few know how to read it. We are conscious that we also wear that sign. It is in our nature. In a competitive society where self-promotion is as common as the air we breathe, we will have little competition at making this empathetic connection once we recognize this sign on those we meet. These people are typically in corporate cultures that do very little to affirm how important they are. Many carry doubts and insecurity about themselves. Anything you do to help people feel more significant will be welcome. The best thing you can do is to make a sincere inquiry.

SELF-CENTERED, SELF-DELUSION

A feature article in the industry magazine *Investment Advisor* (December 2001) described a study that was conducted on the communication skills of investment advisors. The findings, if nothing else, confirmed how easy it is to overestimate one's own empathy skills. Seventy-one percent of respondents in the study said they believed that their clients were content with their communication skills, yet 57 percent of the clients stated that their representative was falling short of their expectations in communication. This tidbit of research points to the silent killer poised to destroy every relationship—believing you are a better communicator than your client thinks you are. It is possible to be the greatest presenter in the company and yet the worst listener. Can you think of such an example? As the relationship progresses, your clients are much more impressed with your listening skills than they are with your presentation skills.

"He just doesn't listen!" were Nancy's words as she explained why she had just changed 401(k) vendors for her company. "I would look this guy in the eye and tell him what I wanted and needed, and yet he would just continue to push on his own agenda. Obviously this was about him and not about us, so we switched. And, technically, he probably has a slightly better product, but I can't deal with the lack of understanding anymore."

It would be difficult to quantify how much money is lost and left on the table because of poor listening skills, but we're quite sure it would be in the billions. On the individual level, we must ask ourselves how much a lack of listening might be costing each of us in our businesses. Is it possible that some of your clients, whom you assume are satisfied with the way you communicate, would say they are not satisfied? The safest premise we can operate from is, *I can always do a better job of listening.* Fanatical curiosity assumes such a posture because we know that this premise will safeguard us from smugness, arrogance, and the sort of hubris that causes important accounts to flee.

Those who possess excellent inquiry skills possess them because they are curious and genuinely interested in others by nature. Yet they have also learned that this skill must be purposefully developed in order to become habitual.

THE EMPATHY REPORT CARD

If your most important client contacts were allowed to grade you on the following listening skills report, how well would you score?

1. My advisor gives his/her undivided attention
   when I am talking.   A B C D F
2. My advisor is tuned into me rather than
   thinking of his/her own response.   A B C D F

3. My advisor answers in a way that reflects my
   major concerns.   A B C D F
4. My advisor keeps conversation focused on my
   needs, issues, and concerns.   A B C D F
5. My advisor summarizes and provides a
   personalized plan for my needs and concerns.   A B C D F

We are all guilty at times of being poor listeners. Some personalities, however, are more susceptible than others. One irony of the sales profession is that the field naturally attracts the enterprising and motivated individuals who, by nature of personality, have short attention spans and are given to impatience—yet their success hinges on their ability to tune in to others. Neither of these features, professional-level ADD or impatience, aids in the development of better listening skills. Sales professionals must constantly check their psychological impulses (picture a hockey "check" here) when interacting with clients.

The fact that we are not all great listeners by nature does not mean we cannot become better listeners and observers. If we approach listening skills as a discipline and a habit, eventually our habit will conquer our impulses. We can develop a pattern that we will feel at home with when engaging in conversation. We simply need a clear agenda for the behaviors that constitute good listening skills.

Here are some of the mistakes that individuals with underdeveloped empathy skills make in conversation.

- They look to make the feature/benefit statements. A chief temptation for sales professionals is to jump too early into a presentation.
- They grandstand with witty comments, stories, and opinions at the expense of the other person's stories and opinions.
- They focus more on facts than on feelings.

- They obsess over details, which causes them to miss the point or the big picture of what the speaker is trying to say.
- They are not in control of nervous or uptight body language signals.
- They focus on their own responses rather than on the person speaking.

Who doesn't occasionally trespass into these boundaries of self-indulgence or self-interest? Tight schedules, demanding goals, and trying clients can combine to take us off our best listening game if we are not vigilant regarding empathetic behavior. Ultimately, it is our discipline in these little matters that defines our destiny.

Ironically, these internal issues and distractions do not dissuade the intensely curious. Why? Because their agendas are different. There is so much that the fanatically curious want to know that they become completely absorbed in the other party's story. The fanatically curious avoid the traps of self-absorption by virtue of "others-absorption." It is not a game. It is not a ploy. They are not asking questions to set up prerecorded monologues—they are asking because they have a real appetite to understand their clients and how they might best be able to help them.

IT'S NOT WHAT YOU TELL BUT WHAT YOU HEAR

Two noticeable patterns of concern in sales training courses are:

1. Overweighted emphasis on presenting with token attention to development of discovery skills
2. Teaching the use of questions and listening as forms of manipulating clients toward a standard sales monologue

The best sales professionals know that more important than having a shoe to sell is first having an accurate measurement of the client's foot, understanding the type of walking the client does, and learning the particular stresses that the client experiences. In other words, they understand the *context* within which they sell. Their context is not, "I have a shoe and you have a foot," but, "You have a need and I may have an answer to that need." Service is based on serving, and the fanatically curious are not prematurely distracted by the fact that they have a nice product to sell.

There is much discovery work that needs to be accomplished in order to ensure a client will be happy with the product. True selling is not in the telling, but in the gathering of information regarding the client. This is why we are focusing on the power of curiosity. Your level of curiosity will determine how much contextual information you gather, how much you understand your clients' motives, how closely you can link their needs with your service, and how long and strong this relationship will become.

DOES CURIOSITY MATTER?

We have made it a point to tell the story of John Sigmund, the top seller described at the beginning of this chapter, in keynotes and seminars for the financial services industry. One interesting reconnection with an audience member has made us grateful that we have shared John's story. A president of a regional bank approached Mitch after a talk and asked, "Do you remember when you presented to our people about a year and a half ago?"

"Yes," Mitch assured him that he remembered, because the talk was in Wisconsin in January.

He continued, "Let me tell you about some conversations I have had just recently about the talk you gave. I asked every broker in our bank system this question, 'In the *StorySelling* presentation, do you remember the story that was told about the top-performing advisor and how he boils his success down to one word? Do you remember the word that he gave?' Interestingly enough," he continued, "the *only* people who could remember the word [curiosity] were our *top performers*."

No surprise there. Top advisors know what this business is all about—the person or persons on the other side of the desk. The more you know about them, the more desire they will have to connect with you.

What makes John Sigmund great at this business is the same thing that made Albert Einstein and Leonardo da Vinci great at their businesses, and it is what will make you great at your business—a deep-seated, insatiable, absolutely have-to-know, *fanatical* curiosity. It was once said of Da Vinci, "He would not take yes for an answer! He always wanted to know more—to get below the surface."

The good news: curiosity is God-given to all of us. It was our natural resting state as children. Curiosity is the reason we put wire hangers in electrical outlets or fingers on hot stoves. (You've done it—admit it!) Somewhere along the line we lost our curiosity. But we can recover it. Curiosity is a memory muscle that can be restored by using it.

You might be saying to yourself, "OK, I'm convinced that success is tied to my curiosity level. I know I need to put the spotlight of conversation on the client and suppress my own narcissistic urges. I want to develop empathy with my clients, but what do I ask?"

Glad you asked. Part II will reveal the types of questions that will help you move from a vendor to a partner in the eyes of your client. But before we get there, let's take a look at why questions are so powerful at the emotional and psychological levels.

2

SIX DEGREES OF SEPARATION

*How You Can Connect
with Anyone . . . Anywhere*

*"Go around asking a lot of damnfool questions and taking chances. Only
through curiosity can we discover opportunities, and only by gambling can we
take advantage of them."*

Clarence Birdseye

Perhaps you have heard of "Six Degrees of
Kevin Bacon"—a parlor game where you try to connect any actor
to Kevin Bacon in less than six degrees. For example, the pioneer-
ing actress Mary Pickford was in *Screen Snapshots* with Clark Gable,
who was in *Combat America* with Tony Romano, who, 35 years later,
appeared in *Starting Over* with Kevin Bacon.

You would probably win the game with this example as it only
took three degrees of separation to connect Mary Pickford and
Kevin Bacon with a connection that spans the entire history of moving pictures. A computer scientist from the University of Virginia
named Brett Tjaden conducted research and found that out of
the approximately 250,000 actors that have ever appeared on television or film, the average degrees of separation from Kevin Bacon
is exactly 2.83! Ponder the implausible odds that there are less than
three degrees of personal connectivity between one actor and every
other actor who has ever participated in the history of the indus-

try. And Kevin Bacon did not even make the top 50 of actors and their connectivity in Tjaden's study.

The top honor goes to Rod Steiger with only 2.6 degrees of separation. Another top ten finisher was Martin Sheen at 2.63 degrees of separation. Studying why Rod Steiger is so closely "connected" to every other actor is instructive for any person seeking to build the connectivity of their own client base. The key to Steiger was the diversity of his career connections. Here is a snapshot of his lifetime in film. He appeared in:

- 38 dramas
- 12 crime pictures
- 11 thrillers
- 8 action films
- 7 westerns
- 6 war films
- 4 documentaries
- 3 horror films
- 2 sci-fi movies
- 1 musical

Steiger starred in enduring classics (*On the Waterfront* and *In the Heat of the Night*, for which he garnered an Oscar), as well as forgettable and pathetic B flicks (anybody remember *Car Pool*?). It is interesting to contrast the "connectivity" of Steiger with that of better-known actors of his age. For example, John Wayne, although he acted in an astounding 179 films, ranked only 116th in the degrees of separation study. This is attributable to the fact that the majority of Wayne's work was in a single genre, the western.

This relationship between broad versus narrow associations, as it relates to connectivity, might cause us to second guess the long-term impact of the "riches in the niches" approach to building a business. A specialization strategy, in the long haul, can have a funneling effect on our connectivity to potential clients. This might explain why so many successful veterans of financial services are working harder for referrals after 20 years in the business than they did in their early years. Is it possible that through specialization they have tapered their field of influence into a demographically constricting pipeline?

Macolm Gladwell, in *The Tipping Point*, his seminal book on achieving critical mass in the marketplace, identified reaching "connectors" as the first leg in the market penetration race. Using the above analysis of "Six Degrees of Kevin Bacon," Gladwell defines connectors as individuals who influence the realms, professions, communities, and neighborhoods in which they circulate. They are people who take special glee and possess special talents for putting together those of like interests and matching people with solutions to people with needs. These individuals can shrink your world and make seemingly improbable connections effortlessly. These connectors, like Rod Steiger, have cultivated broad networks in multiple realms and make the process of connecting seem too facile.

How many degrees of separation do you suppose exist between you and every person of means in your community? How about in the entire United States? The answer might surprise you and raise your awareness of making a conscious effort toward reducing degrees of separation. Amazingly, the study of degrees of separation started in the 1960s with none other than a Boston stockbroker!

In *The Tipping Point*, Gladwell writes about psychologist Stanley Milgram who began seeking answers in the late '60s to what he called the "small world" riddle. He sought to determine if we are all somehow connected and, if so, how? To conduct the study, he employed the use of a chain letter that was given to 160 people chosen randomly out of an Omaha phonebook. Milgram mailed each participant in the study an envelope with the name of a stockbroker from Boston with the instructions to write their name on the envelope and then send the packet to a friend that they thought could get it closer to the Boston broker. For example, if the person in Omaha had a brother-in-law in Springfield, Massachusetts, he would forward it to that individual, and so on.

Intelligent researchers hypothesized that the degrees of separation would be as high as 100. Milgram's study found the actual number to be closer to six; and hence, we have the "six degrees" label to describe the phenomenon of connectivity. Further diagnosis of Milgram's study reveals that a statistically improbable number of connections to the broker came from three gentlemen in the Boston area: Mr. Jacobs, Mr. Brown, and Mr. Jones. Mr. Jacobs, for example, was a clothing merchant who served the broker and was responsible for 16 of the 160 envelopes that eventually made their way to the target.

Who are the connectors in your community? In your field of expertise? How ardent are you in your efforts to make diverse and eclectic connections in your professional and personal associations? Your answers to those questions will undoubtedly determine whether your career navigates in a complex labyrinth "large world" where connections are difficult to find, or a tight-knit and condensed "small world" where connections are always just a phone call or two away.

The degrees of separation phenomenon beckons to the idea that, indeed, "it's a small world after all." Perhaps you too enjoy the irony that this study found its genesis in the linkage of randomly selected Midwesterners to an East Coast financial services professional. Ponder the fact that there are no more than six degrees of separation between you and every potential client in America! The compelling issue, then, is to begin to shrink those degrees of separation. We believe we have found an answer to this contraction challenge with the "Six Degrees" questionnaire presented in the next section.

For the past few years we have been closely studying the questions that top advisors ask in order to establish some common ground or link to the prospect or client before them. We have been on this quest for better questions because we have noted the relational evolution and transformation that takes place when two parties find that they have something in common that was not heretofore revealed. It is a magical sort of rapport, as if some intuitive boundary has been crossed and the travelers look at one another with a knowing glance that says, "You understand, at least in part, my journey."

YOU KNOW WHO?! YOU DID WHAT?!

Scott has been conducting the "Six Degrees" exercise with financial professionals over the last year and has been amazed at the connections that are made—both in a group of randomly gathered individuals and in groups of people that thought they knew each other well. These connections were made simply using "Six Degrees" question cards. The implications of both groups are apparent for the financial services profession: (1) establishing linkage with prospects as soon as possible is critical to their emotional comfort level; and (2) discovering the previously unknown enhances and solidifies existing client relationships.

Mitch once had a major insurance company inquire about using his services. The caller said that his committee was gathering information on possible programs. Rather than just supplying the requested information, Mitch began to inquire about the other members of the decision-making team. Someone mentioned a name that Mitch recognized from his hometown in Iowa. Mitch asked if this gentleman happened to be from Iowa. The caller replied, "Yes, he is!" and mentioned the town in which he had grown up. It was the very same person Mitch thought it was and he told the caller that he had gone to kindergarten with the person! They had a good laugh about that and a small, but important, connection was made.

Connections like these are missed every day in our conversations because we forget to ask background questions.

In the "Six Degrees" exercise Scott has seen people make amazing and intriguing discoveries about common ground. Two people found out that they both shared the hobby of raising albino mice. Two others found out that both of their parents had run catering businesses when they were growing up. (We couldn't shut them up!) Two others found out that they had gone to the same college, belonged to the same fraternity, and shared some of the same professors. Two others discovered that both had missionary grandparents who were forced to flee China in 1949.

Others discovered less profound but still interesting conversation pieces: for example, they had driven the same first car in high school, they grew up idolizing the same hero, or they shared the same childhood movie, book, or television show.

Others found that they had encountered the same change in careers. Others found that they knew some of the same people or shared common experiences that had shaped their lives. It's amazing to witness the odd and interesting connections that get made upon seemingly casual inquiry. Scott and Mitch found out in the course of casual discourse that both had been born cross-eyed, gone through eye operations, and had grown up with wandering eyes. Profound? No. Interesting and memorable? Absolutely. Why? Because it's always refreshing to find another human being who can relate to any part or unusual facet of our lives.

We have discovered that the fanatically curious work hard at asking and finding question paths to explore connections with people. There are many, however, who are curious but just do not know *what* to ask. This is where the question path leading to empathy comes in handy. Following are some of the most successful questions we've discovered for breaking down the degrees of separation.

Questions for Reducing the Six Degrees of Separation

Geography and Culture

1. Where are you from?
2. Where did your parents grow up?
3. What kind of work did your parents do?
4. Where are your family members now?

Vocation and Career Track

5. Where did you go to school?
6. What did you study in college?
7. What was your first job?
8. How did you get from there to here?

Hobbies and Interests

9. What do you like to do in your spare time?
10. Have you traveled much?
11. Where do you like to go?

THE MAP OF LIFE—GEOGRAPHY AND CULTURE

In *StorySelling for Financial Advisors,* we told the story of the advisor who had a map of the United States on his wall and would start every conversation with the question, "Where are you from?" He knew he wasn't asking a geographical question when he posed the question but was opening the door to the world they were from—an exploration of their roots. His map had a stickpin locating the hometown of every client. He would say, "If you can master the discipline of asking that little four-word question and then be quiet, in ten minutes you will be able to see the clear connection between what you offer and their life and experiences."

A prospect and his wife said, "Oh, we're from a little one-horse town in Kansas that you've probably never heard of. Dundee is the name of the town."

Moving to his map full of stickpins, he said, "Can you show me where it's located?" They moved to the board and showed him where Dundee was located. They noticed a stickpin just seven miles away in Great Bend, Kansas, and asked incredulously, "Do you know someone from Great Bend?"

"Oh, that would be Will Smith. He's an engineer over at IBM," the advisor answered.

Mrs. Prospect looked over at Mr. Prospect with a grin and said, "You don't suppose that is John and Sally Smith's boy, do you?"

"It must be," says Mr. Prospect. "I only knew of one Will Smith from Great Bend."

"I'll be glad to ask him and mention that I met you folks," the advisor offered.

This advisor has witnessed the melting of degrees of separation many times with this one simple question about their beginnings. He loves this exercise because of the way it illustrates the "small world" principle. Once they discover that you share a common acquaintance or familiarity, the degrees of separation begin to melt away.

What are the odds, in asking where they are from, that you will know someone from that area? Slim. What are the odds that you will be familiar with someone who is from that area? Better. What are the odds that you will know someone from that area if you are in the habit of asking everyone you meet where they are from? Much better.

NOT ABOUT GEOGRAPHY

The next time you inquire into someone's roots, note the natural pattern of the conversation. Without prompting, people will often volunteer stories or facts of "what life was like in . . ." This demonstrates the point that Where are you from? is less a geography question than a cultural inquiry. With just a touch of interviewing skill, you can transform the "Where are you from?" question into a microcosmic view of the life and core-values of the person you are getting to know. For the truly curious this question of beginnings easily leads to:

"What was life like there?"

"Do you still have any family there?"

"Do you ever get back there?"

Such conversations are enjoyable and beneficial. People, for reasons that are not totally explicable, enjoy reminiscing and appreciate the opportunity to explain their roots. For you, the curious listener, it is a magic window into the essence of who they are and how they see themselves. To their peers they may be John the lawyer, but in their hometown they were Johnny on Elm Street who swam the backstroke for the swim team, delivered papers for many years, and dated the math teacher's daughter. After hundreds of such conversations, I have come to suspect that lying latent within most people, especially professionals, is a desire to have others discover who they really are. Their job requires that they put on a certain level of professionalism, which provides little opportunity for unguarded self-disclosure.

As your biographical process begins, allow it to flow into other aspects of their background, such as a description of their parents, their parents' work, the dispersion of their family now, and the whereabouts and careers of their siblings and extended family. It won't be long before you make a connection.

The "Six Degrees" inquiry flows naturally into your clients' work interests and career history: where they first started their career efforts, the bends and detours in their career paths, the story of how they got from there to here, the people and circumstances that connect them to their current stations in life, and their occupational hopes for the future. Who knows, it may be you that connects them to someone who helps them make the next step on their road map of life! If you behave like a connector, statistically it is bound to happen.

Outside of family and work connectors, you can make meaningful connections in leisure activities and pleasure pursuits, such as golf, racquetball, cooking classes, and curling clubs. A recent study about why people have the social networks and friends they do revealed a disconnect between people's perceptions about the reason for their social connections and the *real* reason. People think they have the connections because they share the same attitudes and philosophies; further inquiry, however, showed that they share the same *activities!*

Take time to inquire into your clients' hobbies, travels, and pleasure pursuits. By doing so, you will no doubt make some connections. Chances are you will know some place, some person, or some experience that they have known.

We believe that the only thing separating you from any client is a lack of curiosity or the right questions. Get to know as much as you can about everyone you meet. Seek to be the Rod Steiger of your profession by making connections in every way possible. You will find out that the smaller your world, the larger the dividends.

3

WHY WE CAN'T RESIST
A GREAT QUESTION
11 Reasons to Stop Telling and Start Asking

"Curiosity killed the cat, but for a while I was a suspect."

Steven Wright

Have you ever watched the Sunday morning political talk shows where there are four or five political columnists, all brimming over with opinions to the point that none of them can let any of the others finish a thought without being interrupted? This game of "opinionous interruptus" reaches its climax on each respective issue when the host offers an opinion-ending pontification with a tone that implies, "This thought is so final and incisive that there is no need to discuss this issue any further."

Everybody is talking and nobody is really listening; they're just waiting for their turn to talk. People are fighting for the spotlight and hoping to be seen as the authority. It sounds an awful lot like the typical meeting or conversation. The conversations you enter into today may likely have the same emotional undercurrents that we see animated in an over-the-top fashion on these political debate shows:

- People want to be heard.
- People want their opinions to be appreciated.
- People enjoy having the spotlight.
- Control of a conversation requires talking.

If you've ever had a conversation where the other party couldn't ask enough questions about you, where you felt like you were talking to a biographer who was trying to capture the essence of your life and your world, you would certainly remember that conversation. Those sorts of conversations are so rare that most of us can count the number we have had in our lifetimes on one hand. Many tell us that they cannot remember ever having such a conversation.

It stands to reason that if you are the individual stimulating these sorts of conversations with your clients, *you* will be the one standing out—like one tall stalk of wheat among a field bowed together by the winds of narcissism. It's easy to identify the true curious, those truly interested in us, the truly engaged conversationalists in our lives. There are so few of them. The attention grabbing, "notice me and my wit," "I'll one-up that story," self-orbiting conversationalists, however, are lost in a sea of faces.

Scott was curious about Socrates, the famous Greek philosopher whose life was marked by asking the right questions. Scott did an online search for what was written by Socrates about the Socratic method. There was nothing! Socrates simply practiced what he preached—it was implicit in his method.

INTELLIGENCE'S INQUIRY

There are many good reasons for becoming a person with a reputation for asking good questions. The selfish reason is, of course, that being an intelligent inquirer will help your image. People respect the asker and listener more than they respect the teller and seller. Selfishly speaking, intelligent inquiry also elevates other people's opinion of your intellect and capabilities—unless, of course, you ask stupid questions. They figure you are asking because you know what you are doing.

Where we will focus this chapter, however, is on the benefits for your clients as you ask intelligent questions. We will offer 11 outstanding benefits to your clients as you make intelligent and relevant inquiry. Revealed in the following pages are the true powers of questions analyzed through an emotional and psychological filter. Once you've finished this chapter, you'll not only think twice before dominating any conversation but you will be fascinated by observing the impact your questions have on your audience.

THE POWER OF QUESTIONS

The Internal Benefits

Benefit 1: A good question allows people their space on the stage of life. Imagine that your office is a stage on which is being played out a drama on personal finance. The narrator describes the setting, the lights come up, and the spotlight finds the lead actor who is your client. You are the supporting actor in this script. If you keep in mind your true role, you will realize that most of your good lines in this script are intelligent questions, not clever witticisms or brilliant sales pitches.

Have you ever realized that people want to be noticed? People not only want to be noticed, they want to be recognized, affirmed, respected, even admired. One workplace study revealed that being recognized more often was more important to most workers than being paid more. One of the greatest favors you can do for any person is to establish at the very beginning of the conversation where your spotlight is pointed. Not only will they be flattered that you are interested in them and their world, they will warm to you in the glow of that spotlight.

Benefit 2: Inquiry elevates *their* intellect and reason.

"Even a fool, when he holds his peace is counted wise: he that shuts his lips is esteemed a man of understanding."

Proverbs 17:28

"Better to remain silent and be thought a fool than to open your mouth and remove all doubt"

Abraham Lincoln

Do you ever notice the types of people that tend to dominate conversations? They often are people who are in love with the sound of their own voice and can't hear enough of their own opinions. They often start with, "What do you think about such and such?" and before you can put together two sentences of response, they interrupt with, "Well, I'll tell you what I think . . ." and proceed to demonstrate just how highly they think of what they think.

They are completely clueless as to the boredom they bring!

When you do the asking instead of the telling, you elevate the intellect, reason, and thoughts of the other party. Rare is the person who will resist your attempts to understand them—their thoughts and ideas, and how they came by them. There are too few inquirers in this arena; those who master this habit will find that people are unaccustomed to being interviewed in a manner that Barbara Walters saves for very important people.

Somebody actually cares to know *what* I think and *why* I think the way I think. Now there's a shocker.

Benefit 3: Intelligent inquiry recognizes an individual's uniqueness. Talk to any publisher and you'll hear them lament over how many novice writers think they have a story to tell. Look at the growth of self-publishing and the companies that exist to help capture your story on audio or video and one fact emerges: everyone *does* have a story to tell.

While every person's story may not be interesting to others, it is interesting to them—and they want to tell it. The problem is that not many people want to sit and hear the stories. Even more unusual is the individual that attempts to cajole the story out of people. The advisor who acts as biographer will find that clients feel more connected and loyal to the financial professional who cares enough to seek out and listen to their personal biography.

Rick is an advisor in Canada who uses Mitch's Financial Life Planning (FLP) system for gathering biographical information on clients. In the FLP system, there are a few profiles that the client fills out and the rest is intended for the advisor to fill in after qualitative inquiry with the client. Against Mitch's advice, Rick decided to send the entire biographical workbook to his clients to fill out regarding history, current life transitions, principles, and future goals. Mitch thought it would be too daunting for a client to have to fill in all the answers outside the flow and framework of a conversation.

What Rick found, however, was that he was getting back over 90 percent of the workbooks *completely* filled out and returned before the clients even came in for their meeting. They told Rick that they loved the process of telling their stories—where they were from, what it was like growing up, what they wanted to be, and what they became. They wanted to share information about their lives, about the challenges and opportunities they faced, and about the values and principles they followed in helping their families, lives, and investments to grow. It was as close as most people will ever get to actually writing a book about their lives. This desire stored in the heart of the earliest human to the most recent is what we will call the *autobiographical urge*.

Great things lie in store for the advisor who acts as biographer and discovers the story lines that make each client unique.

Benefit 4: Questions reveal priorities and issues of import.

Questions reveal personal land mine and gold mine stories. What is your earliest recollection of memory? What would your client be talking about if you weren't doing the talking? Probably about an issue they felt was important. One advisor told us the story of how he gave a sterling presentation of a secondary offering in a bio-tech company, which he felt was a great opportunity. The gentleman, to whom he was presenting this opportunity for 15 minutes, looked at him at the end of the presentation and said, "No way!" The advisor asked him why he felt that way about this investment opportunity. The man replied, "My brother-in-law lost his shirt in bio-tech when the FDA failed to approve a drug."

This advisor lamented, "I wish I'd asked how he felt about annuities *before* I gave my brilliant presentation." Agreed. We will always find ourselves further ahead as a result of asking than we will by telling. An important feature of asking well-thought-out questions is that we help clients sift through their own priorities and force them to decide what is important enough to act upon.

The revealing question can be as benign as What is it that brings you here today?, which is where a good doctor would start an examination with a patient. Advisors have been taught to focus on possibilities (goals) and miss the opportunities that lie in helping people manage financial pain and financial priorities.

Here are some questions to stimulate clients in sorting out their priorities.

- What is the most important financial issue in your life at this moment?
- What is going on in your life right now that could have a major financial impact?
- What do you see as the biggest threat to your financial security?
- If you had all the money you would ever need, what issue would you first address?
- What do you want your money to do for you?

Questions like these are used effectively by advisors to assist clients in the process of figuring out what matters most—which, in the process of advising, matters most.

Benefit 5: Good questions raise personal awareness and often help save clients from themselves. Most of us don't have to look much further than the bathroom mirror to see someone who has done something really stupid with his or her money. There are very few people who do not have a "Here's how I threw hard-earned money down a sinkhole" testimony. We all have vulnerabilities regarding our money. Some of us, however, are aware of our vulnerabilities; others are only subconsciously aware and continue to fall into the same self-sabotaging money patterns.

With some it is the mismanagement of debt. With others it is the inability to say no to a too-good-to-be-true idea from the "opportunities" page in the want ads or from an associate hyping his latest stake-claim. With others it is the inability to organize their records and bring logic to their overall plan. Others lack diversification, while some are in complete denial of their disjointed financial state.

Good questions can help to raise destructive financial habits and patterns to the surface and provide an opportunity to show your clients how to form constructive money habits.

One advisor asked a client about recollections regarding money and the client shared his story of being cheated out of money as a child by a relative. It became crystal-clear to this advisor why this client was never willing to act on his advice. He suspected everyone was trying to cheat him. After they talked about his hypersuspicion issues, the client starting taking his advice and working for—instead of against—his own best interests.

The External (Relational) Benefits

Benefit 6: Good questions have a disarming effect. During the bear market that ushered in this new century, many advisors feared the client conversation. Brian was not one of those advisors. He saw the situation for what it really was—an unprecedented opportunity for taking client relationships to a new and deeper level. He told us, "This is the greatest bull market in history . . . for building client relationships. Most advisors are so paralyzed by their clients' disappointment and anger that they are afraid to have a conversation. I'm offering them the conversation they want."

The problem or challenge was that clients were coming in with visible emotional distress. They wanted counsel more than they wanted advice on what to do next with their money. They anticipated a battle or a debate, and so they were defensive in their posture. Brian recognized their fears and disarmed them immediately by asking, "What effect has this market downturn had on you, and how do these reports of corruption affect you?" It was not a question so much as an invitation. It gave clients permission to unload their frustration and disappointment. It disarmed the tension they might have expected in this meeting.

His next question was, "What lessons have you learned from what we have just been through?" Invariably the lesson they learned was tied to having a new respect for risk tolerance. At this point Brian would introduce this idea: "What I have learned is that when we focus only on great potential returns, this focus can turn to great potential losses when the market storm rises against us. I've learned that we need to start focusing on what you need this money for in your life, and to only take the risks that make sense. In other words, if you don't need this money for 25 years, it makes sense to leave it in the equities market where it has a better chance to grow in the long run. But if you need this money in seven years, we need to use more protective measures and take steps to ensure that your money will be there when you need it."

Brian then began to inquire what his clients ultimately needed the money for, and established a new context for the investment choices they would make going forward. He was able to disarm the negativity of past events and begin the rebuilding process. A great secret of top advisors who prospered during this market downturn was their willingness to allow clients to express their feelings of what had happened to them.

When prospective clients walk in to an office expecting to be "sold" and the advisor begins asking questions, it begins to disarm their tension over being "sold." People hold on to that tension until it becomes apparent through the line of questioning that the advisor is there to serve a legitimate need and not to push a product.

Benefit 7: Biographical inquiry reveals possible connection points. In Chapter 2, "Six Degrees of Separation," you discovered that connections are easy to find if you ask enough questions. Although it would be difficult to make a meaningful connection with every person we meet, the lack of connection that we sense with many people is the result of a lack of inquiry effort on our part. If we *seek* a connection point we can usually find one. It may be someone we both know, a hobby we share, a place we have been, a book we have read, a view we share, a common faith, an experience we've had, commonalities growing up, our parents' jobs, or one of many other points of connection on our respective maps of life.

If you view your role as a biographer first and as an advisor second, you will invariably find connections with every client. If you view yourself as a salesperson of financial products, you will unwittingly speed past common ground and miss the opportunity to connect. It doesn't take long to find a connection. It starts with questions about where they are from and doesn't end until we know where it is they would like to end up.

Benefit 8: Good questions turn conversations into a fascinating journey instead of a "death march." Have you ever seen excitement in the eyes and the anticipation on the faces of your clients when you hand them your "discovery forms?" Probably not. The forms most likely contain quantitative, fact-based questions your clients may have answered scores of times and questions they'd rather not answer in the first place. Walking through most questionnaires we have seen is akin to participating in a statistical death march.

The death march could be traded in for a fascinating journey by making it an actual "personal discovery" session instead of a march to gather numbers, facts, and account balances. Anybody can fill out forms but not everybody can engage a client in a meaningful way. The difference between "death march" discovery and a fascinating journey is in the quality of the qualitative questions you ask.

Benefit 9: Questions unlock the memory bank. We have heard much about the aging of America and the graduating gray tint to wealth in our society. Ken Dychtwald reports that over 60 percent of all people in the history of the world who have lived past 65 are alive right now. And people over the age of 60 control over 70 percent of the wealth. Did you also know that when people get close to 60 their brain's functionality moves from left-side rationalizing more to right-side intuiting?

While the short-term memory function occasionally goes on tilt in the left side of the brain, the long-term memory bank is a virtual warehouse of experiences and reference points. A key to making an emotional connection with any client—especially those in this age group—is engaging in conversations that unlock the memory bank.

The power of reminiscence is a strange but powerful phenomenon. We scholastically know very little about reminiscence but intuitively realize that it is a cohesive element in friendship and bonding. Reminiscence causes people to reach back into the storehouse of significant experience and draw out the moments and lessons that have made an impact in their lives. Well-designed questions stimulate this reminiscing process and allow clients to open up areas of discovery that would otherwise go unrevealed. A key to building lasting client relationships is not just knowing where clients want to go but knowing where they've been.

Benefit 10: Questions allow the client to be the copilot instead of the passenger. Too often in presentations clients feel like passengers that are being "taken for a ride." The time has come for financial services presentations to evolve from narrow monologues into meaningful dialogues. By asking questions, you encourage your prospects or clients to espouse their opinions, tell their stories, or articulate their hopes. In effect, you are handing over the wheel to them. You are like the driver education teacher who sits in the front passenger seat and has a brake pedal in case the driver gets too far off course. In that case, you simply ask another question that brings you back to a path where something constructive can be accomplished.

Benefit 11: You may actually learn something. A financial planner who attended our workshop on better client discovery wrote to us a few days after the training and said, "I had always taken great pride in how well I know my clients and the quality of our relationship. You could never have convinced me before this training experience that I didn't know them well enough. But when I used some of the questions and inquiry paths you suggested, I began to learn details about 15-year clients that I did not know— important details that a financial planner needs to know, details that could cause the best financial plan in the world to unravel at any moment if not addressed."

Great minds have always looked for better questions because they are intensely curious. Einstein wanted to know. Da Vinci wanted to know. You want to know. Great discovery emanates from an authentic well of curiosity. It's not about simply asking questions. It's about knowing what it is you want to know and designing questions that will draw those stories out.

In the next chapters we explain what we need to know to forge a partnership and to truly serve the good of our clients.

4

INTERESTED, NOT INTERESTING
Find Out What Makes Each Client Unique

"Everyone has a story to tell but few have had the opportunity to tell it."

Anon

"Children show no respect and everybody wants to be a writer."

Unknown, from a papyrus containing the oldest piece of literature known on earth

A method for recording and preserving ideas (other than cave scribblings) had just been discovered and one of the first writers laments the fact that everyone thinks they have a story to tell and that they "ought to write a book." We wish we could have a nickel for each time someone has walked up to us and said, "You know, I've thought of writing a book," and a quarter for every time someone has said, "Hey, maybe we should write a book together!" Mitch was at a New Year's Eve party and was introduced to a gentleman who said, "Didn't you write a book called *The New Retirementality*?" Mitch lit up anticipating an intriguing discussion about his book. He responded, "Yes, have you read it?" The gentleman said, "No I haven't, but you know I've had a very interesting life myself. Tell me a little about the process of writing a book."

While every person's story may not be interesting to you, it is interesting to that individual—and he or she wants to tell it. The problem is, not many people want to sit and hear another person's story. Even rarer is the individual who attempts to cajole the story out of someone. The advisor who acts as biographer will find that clients feel quite connected and loyal to a person who cares enough to seek and hear their personal biography. We believe that a greatly underappreciated, powerful driving force in every human is the need to be *known*.

Mitch once met an advisor who told him that he wasn't satisfied with any conversation with new acquaintances until he knew some fact of their life that made them unique—something that he would easily remember about them. Contrast this conversational attitude with the banal majority of people who aren't satisfied with a conversation until they have told you a dozen interesting facts about themselves.

WHERE ARE YOU FROM?

After presenting a StorySelling keynote speech (where we always talk about asking people where they are from), Mitch was approached by an advisor who had a story to tell.

"A few months back I was invited to attend a cocktail party at a local old folks' home in Little Rock," he started. "Now I know you're wondering about my social life—and I wondered too as I walked into the event. But it ended up being one of the most fascinating nights of my life."

He sat down in a circle of people, all of whom were in their 70s to 90s, and asked the woman next to him, "Where did you grow up?" She told him the exact address. He nearly fell out of his chair. It was the exact address at which he had once lived when he was renting a small house in the back of the property. They had some great laughs and conversation about that old house and the various people that had lived in it through the years.

He then asked her where she had gone after she moved out of that house. She told him about going to a nearby college where she had roomed with the famous poet, Edna St. Vincent Millay. "How fascinating," the advisor thought, as she described their relationship.

At this point, he began to notice a woman a couple of chairs down who seemed quite tuned in to their conversation. "How about you?" he asked. "Where are you from?"

"Oh me," she replied, "I'm from Wisconsin."

"Really?" he responded. "What did you do in Wisconsin?"

"Oh, I worked for the government," she replied dismissively.

"What did you do with the government?" he inquired further.

"I worked for a United States senator," she said as nonchalantly as possible.

"And which senator was that?" the advisor asked.

"Senator Joseph McCarthy," she informed him. They had a most interesting conversation about those days and what it was like to be on the inside of the most historical period of communistic paranoia.

The advisor then noticed a fellow in the circle had been eavesdropping, so he turned to him and asked, "Well, what's your story?"

"I was an educator," he said.

"Not just any educator," one of the ladies offered.

"Where were you an educator, and what did you do?" the advisor asked.

"I was a superintendent of schools right here in Little Rock," he answered.

Then it struck the advisor that there may be another historical figure right there in that small circle. "Were you the school superintendent in 1955?" he queried, referring to the date of the historical civil rights event of the color line being broken at an all-white high school.

"I certainly was," he answered, and they proceeded to have yet another amazing conversation. Needless to say this "geriatric happy hour" turned out to be one of the best parties this advisor had ever wandered into. What are the odds of encountering three such amazing stories in one place in Little Rock? The former roommate of a famous poet, a secretary to a famous and historically significant senator, and a famous figure in the battle for civil rights! Amazing.

What struck this advisor that night was the number of other amazing stories he has failed to hear because he failed to ask and failed to show interest. That's the part that gets to us. How many wonderful, beautiful, interesting, and amazing stories do we walk right by in the average week?"

THE AUTOBIOGRAPHICAL IMPULSE

Not only does every person have a story to tell, he or she also has a need to tell it. Granted, you won't always hear dramatic histories like this advisor did, but you will hear stories of importance because each person is important and has a unique story. Ponder this possibility: you may be the first person who has ever asked. Most people focus on being interesting rather than showing genuine interest in another. We all have a biographical impulse that fuels a parade of stories about ourselves; yet we somehow fail to connect the need to tell our own story to the fact that others harbor the same impulse.

This is especially true of recent retirees who feel they are experiencing a loss of respect and a horrid societal demotion. As one retiree put it, "I went from being in *Who's Who* to 'Who's he?' almost overnight." These retirees are suffering from what Mitch calls Loss of Status Syndrome (LOSS). Suddenly they feel they are no longer valued. Because they aren't "doing" anything, they feel their story means little or nothing. We will not outgrow or "outmature" this need for respect. Curiosity is the ultimate form of respect; it states: Your story is important to me.

The autobiographical impulse lives within us all. It is the neglected key that unlocks meaningful and lasting client relationships. We remember and are loyal to the people who show an interest in us.

AMAZING PEOPLE

Would you like to be remembered by others as an amazing person? It won't happen by dominating conversations but by leading them—and leading them away from yourself. Mitch loves to tell the story of two such amazing people he met as a result of his brother Mark's curiosity.

While his brother was in college studying political science, he came across two books in the college library by Evelyn Lincoln, the former secretary to John F. Kennedy entitled, *Kennedy and Johnson* and *My Twelve Years with JFK*. Mark was an aficionado of JFK, reading everything he could get his hands on, and was thrilled to come across these two old volumes that had not been checked out of the library in over 15 years.

Mark decided to write Mrs. Lincoln a letter to tell her how much he enjoyed her books. Much to his surprise she wrote back a lengthy letter. She was in her 70s by then and not many people paid any further attention to her books—or to John F. Kennedy for that matter—and she was thrilled to find a student so curious and interested. The letter exchange soon turned into a telephone exchange and then an invitation to come and visit Evelyn and her husband, Harold, who had worked closely with Bobby Kennedy in the Attorney General's office. Needless to say, Mark was ecstatic.

After a couple of visits, Mark invited Mitch to come out and meet these most interesting people and rare sources of modern American historical insight. Mitch gives this account:

"The dinner, which started at 6:00 PM, didn't wrap up until midnight, and was peerless in my life in terms of intrigue and interest in a dinner conversation. Here sat two very important and knowledgeable historical figures who were on the inside of the Bay of

Pigs, the Cuban missile crisis, the assassination, etc., and yet their knowledge and insight was largely neglected. They lived on the inside of history and had stories to tell—awe-inspiring, revelatory, and salacious.

"As intriguing as this conversation was, the most astounding component of the conversation to me was the fact that I had never met two people in my life who showed more interest in me. Here I am, an unknown young man from Iowa, and these two interviewed me like my story was the greatest account they had ever heard. They found out unique aspects of my life, work, and ideas—and kept digging like archeologists who found a valuable shard. I was dumbfounded at their genuine interest in me, contrasted with whom they were and their status in the world compared with mine."

"I felt like I had to wrestle my way out of their interest in me to get them to share their endlessly interesting stories and insights on 'people inside the beltline.'"

"If we ever told the things we know, it would blow the lid off Capital Hill," Harold told us—and they would have. Evelyn had kept a journal of JFK's whereabouts and doings from 1951 to 1963 and had been offered millions by publishers for it. She never sold it and took it to her grave.

These people still stand out in Mitch's memory as two of the most amazing people he has ever met, not just because of whom they were, but also because of how interested they were in who he was.

EARNING REAL CLIENT INTEREST

In our presentations we urge our audiences to begin showing more interest in their clients' lives. Afterwards, advisors often approach us and ask, "If I have neglected to do this in the past, isn't it going to seem sort of strange to start going deeper into their story now?"

Our answer: "Only if you are uncomfortable asking."

What do you feel when people show genuine interest in your life, history, work, and accomplishments? Offended? Invaded? No. That's what you feel when people ask inappropriate, prying, or silly psychological questions. When you inquire about their story, an altogether dissimilar dynamic enters the conversation. The emotions of being interesting, worthy of inquiry, and important enter and dialogue rolls forth. In the process, you gain a real appreciation for whom you are working, and that empathetic connection is so powerful that it will be next to impossible for any competitor to wedge between you and your client.

If you have been conducting fairly superficial conversations with your clients, try moving the conversation toward a keen interest in their story the next time you meet. You can start by saying, "I don't know if I ever asked you before, but where are you from?" or, "How did you get started in this line of work?" or, "How did you two meet?" If an icy glare develops between the couple after that last question, back off immediately!

Show interest in their children's stories. Show interest in their parents' stories. You'll begin to understand a tacit but tried law of successful business relationships: *the more interest you show in me the more interested I become in working with you.*

A CHANGE IN EMOTION

Can genuine interest change a negative client into an appreciative client or even a fan? Can empathy transform antipathy into affection? Unless it has been a breach of trust, we believe it can.

Back in 2000 at an industry luncheon in Washington D.C., an advisor shared an account with us of how he was invited by a buddy to a private fundraiser for a local candidate where Bill Clinton was going to be present. This advisor's friend knew that he was the king of Clinton-haters when he invited him, but at $250 a ticket and the opportunity to be one of only 30 people present, his friend felt that it was too good to pass up and refused to take no for an answer.

This advisor went with his feet dragging, but with sufficient curiosity. He didn't like Clinton's politics, didn't like his views, and loathed his character. He only went because his friend went to the effort, and he wanted to be able to say he met the former president.

They walked into the kitchen and there was Bill Clinton leaning against the stove chatting it up with a handful of people. This advisor was immediately struck by how big a man he was—around six feet four inches. Clinton was a commanding presence in the room, even without being president. The advisor was introduced and the former president turned to him and began making all manner of inquiry into whom he was, what he did, etc. For the next five minutes Clinton treated him like he was the most important citizen in the country, and that he couldn't learn enough about him.

This advisor was literally blown away by Clinton's manner and charisma. He told us that he couldn't remember someone this important ever being so intensely focused on him. He then understood Bill Clinton's immense appeal. In a matter of minutes Clinton had turned him from a stalwart opponent to an admirer, in spite of what he knew.

STORIES TO TELL

Are you a student of the human experience? Like the advisor we mentioned earlier, are you unsatisfied with a conversation until you grasp something significant and unique about the person with whom you're conversing? Amazing stories are waiting to be unearthed—excavated if you will—and to have their true worth discovered, one shard at a time. The problem is that there is a vast shortage of archeologists.

Start digging. There's no telling what you'll find.

5

THE QUESTION *IS* THE ANSWER

Moving from Monologues to Dialogues

"Only the curious will learn and only the resolute overcome the obstacles to learning. The Quest Quotient has always excited me more than the intelligence quotient."

Eugene Wilson

Our friend Gary has been in the financial services business most of his life, and so he understands the sales side of the business inside and out. Recently he had some real concerns about risk management and asset protection going forward and decided to call for an appointment with a representative from a large insurance company. Gary told us about this insightful experience.

The sales representative came into his office, well dressed and with a very professional carriage. He did a quick scan of Gary's walls and did the "Dale Carnegie thing" making some small talk about kids, family, etc. He then focused on Gary and asked him, "So, Gary, where do you see yourself five years from today?"

Gary said that every cell in his emotional system instantly shut down. The conversation was over at that point because, being trained in sales, he knew he had been trained to ask that question and it felt so artificial—what we would characterize as a synthetic question.

Synthetic is a very good word to describe many of the questions employed by sales organizations to provoke conversations leading to their products and services. With a little creativity and intuitive insight, they could reach the same end with genuine and authentic lines of questioning that uncover the needs and opportunities in the client's life.

Gary later told us that what he found so exasperating about the synthetic line of questioning was that the issues he faced—protecting his family, his lifestyle, and the assets built up over 30 years—were serious financial and emotional concerns to him. Not only did the sales representative turn him off with this artificial approach to his very serious life concerns, he completely missed the point! Gary had called to talk about protecting what he had, not dreaming about some place down the road.

We sensed in Gary's story the atomic collision between the synthetic and the sacred.

THE QUESTION AS A TOOL OF MANIPULATION

As Scott was doing research for the development of a keynote speech entitled, *FIN'atical Curiosity,* he pored over the books in the sales marketplace that purported to teach professionals how to ask questions in order to become better at their trade. Scott found books that promised to teach how to become more skilled at asking questions but were actually tomes on sophisticated emotional manipulation—if you ask *this,* and they say *this,* then you say *this.* These questions are not questions at all. They are thinly veiled assertions. They are imposters for true curiosity. If you ask, "If I could show you a product that will do . . . ?" you are not asking a question, you are setting up a soapbox. If you ask, "It's probably time to diversify, don't you think?" you are telling or selling but you are not asking.

The authors of said question paths—and, subsequently, their readers—miss the point entirely. This prosaic, self-serving sort of inquiry uses questions only to rip off the rind in order to get their hands on the fruit, tearing it apart cling by cling, while the seeds of true opportunity fall to the ground waiting for another advisor to harvest. They do employ questions, but only as a means to set up the statements, and there will be more than a few of those coming! We have found that clients will not only invest the fruit of their labors with you but also the groves of opportunity that exist in the seeds if you ask the right questions for the right reasons.

We cannot call it "discovery" if nothing is discovered.

Discovery is an aberration when curiosity is absent. Curiosity prefers to know the client rather than control the client. Curiosity will always choose the best question path because curiosity's chief aim is to unlock the code of whom a client is, not to get the combination to his or her safe-deposit box.

Manipulations abound in the marketplace—and clients continue to develop better radar toward each new manifestation of these manipulations. Living in an age where consumers are taught to question the sincerity of every recommendation should be enough to ward off those given to the temptation to push products through questions that are not questions at all. But, alas, it is not.

Those who are willing to resort to manipulation as a sales tactic may also be enticed to use bullying, intimidation, and fear tactics as well. These advisors—and the firms they represent—soon find themselves on the wrong end of the fiduciary measuring stick. Asking manipulative questions is not only bad for the client, it's bad for the business.

THE 100 PERCENT ADVISOR

Mitch's firm, Advisor Insights, Inc., has been studying the impact of discovery methodologies on the percentage of assets under management for the last two years. What they have discovered is that the industry average (across all channels) for investable assets under management for the average advisor-client relationship is in the neighborhood of 30 percent to 35 percent. As a contrast to this industry average, we sought out advisors and planners who have a "100 percent relationship" with their average client so we could compare the discovery methods and engagement models. The contrasts were, to say the least, glaring. Here are some observations.

The 35 Percent Advisor	The 100 Percent Advisor
Engages in financial monologues	Engages in dialogues
Conversations center on product or service	Conversations revolve around the client's life
Money is the "client"	Client is the client

What is a financial monologue? It is asking a question you already know the answer to (or presume to know the answer to) for the purposes of launching a presentation that you planned on launching before you ever asked the question. Mitch could not find 100 percent advisors that used this sort of technique. These advisors were engaged in dialogues that were centered on the life of the client and the financial implications of what was going on in that life. A dialogue starts by asking a question you don't know the answer to and entering into a very real and genuine flow of conversation that is based on the answers you hear.

The word *dialogue* comes from the Greek word *dialogos*, which means the "flow of meaning." This is the true essence of beneficial conversation—both parties' interests merge into one stream of meaning and purpose. (By the way, the Greek word *monologos* means "one meaning," which makes one wonder whose meaning is being served in such a conversation!)

Another observation we made is that the 35 percent advisor is in the "what" business—where the true client is not the client but the money that the client controls. We can't help but wonder what a client would think if he overheard his advisor refer to him as "my $2 million client." With the 100 percent crowd, there is a definitive distinction here because they acknowledge that they have learned that this is a "who" business and that the assets are always entrusted with the individual who best understood the "who." Once clients feel their advisors understand them and the soul of their motives, moving the money over is a natural course of progression.

You can move from a 35 percent relationship to a 100 percent relationship in a matter of an hour with a turn of the heart and the right question. This "turn of the heart" involves becoming honest with yourself about your motives in client conversations. As the following story illustrates, no one is exempt from the temptation of placing self-interest at the core and client service at the periphery.

One advisor sent Mitch an e-mail two days after she attended his financial life dialogues training. She admitted how selfish she had been in client conversations over the years. Thoughts of how she could "cash in" on these conversations had always been there lurking. After the workshop, she tested what she had learned by asking one of her clients, "What's going on in your life right now that could have a serious effect on your financial future?"

Her client immediately began to pour out the story of her brother who is fighting a life-threatening disease. He couldn't work and his entire family had rallied around him, financially and emotionally. This advisor was very moved by her dedication to her brother. In the course of listening to her heartrending story, the advisor learned a great deal about her client's background and family.

She wrote that about 30 minutes into the conversation the strangest thing happened. Her client looked at her and told her how she was the only one who really understood her situation, and that she wanted to move all her money over to her.

This brought the advisor close to tears. She had been trying her whole career to get people to move money to her without a lot of success. She realized for the first time that when a financial professional's motivation truly becomes about the clients and their lives, both the clients and the money follow.

This is the lesson that the 100 percent advisor has embraced. Yet, the industry is still fighting the impact of the product-focused, self-interested monologues that abound.

ARE YOU INTERESTED IN A PERSON OR A PERSONAL INTEREST?

Mitch received a phone call from an advisor, Mick, because a mutual friend had told Mitch about an extremely competitive loan he had received and mentioned that he might be interested in the same. Using this friend as a reference, Mick made a cold call to Mitch, beginning his pitch with the following exchange:

"So, you're a friend of Tommy?" he asked.

"Yes," Mitch answered. "I don't know if we have ever met."

"You belong to the golf club, don't you?" Mick asked.

"Yeah, sure do."

"How's the game?" he asked.

"Oh, you know, up and down," Mitch answered.

"You wrote a book, didn't you?" Mick asked.

"Actually, I've written a number of books," Mitch replied.

"Yeah, yeah right," Mick replied, trying to keep himself from having to go down any dialogue path other than the one he intended for this call. "So, regarding this loan, let me ask you, how much do you have in equities?"

Almost too stunned to answer, Mitch began to mentally assemble all that had been communicated in Mick's short, disastrous reply: "I have no interest in you personally," "I'm cutting to the chase and want to know if it is worth my while to talk to you," "I do deals and don't bother with any of the warm, fuzzy stuff that might slow them down."

Tommy, the friend that referred Mitch to Mick later told about being humiliated by him at a golf outing. Surrounded by his peers, Mick had asked Tommy how his loan was coming along. Tommy was in the midst of his answer when Mick cut him off and said, "You know, I've already spent more time on this than I do on my $5 million clients. Call me on Monday." Translation: "You're not very important."

Mick is a stark example of those individuals, who, by their manner and conversation pattern, give the impression that they do this business purely out of personal interests as opposed to an interest in persons. Few people in the financial industry are as blatant as Mick in exhibiting self-interest, but that does not mean self-interest is not the trump card for many other conversations taking place. We would advise any professional to take a close and scrutinizing look at your chosen conversation structure and weigh the emotional signals you may be sending to the client.

We understand that most professionals would not take the abbreviated and desultory jump from asking about a client's golf game to account balances in a nanosecond. Mick defied his pressing interest in a matter of seconds. Others can be subtler but their conversation pattern gives them away in the end. Clients have their antennae up and are using their emotional radar to read the imperative that drives the conversation for you, the professional.

FIRST DATES

Imagine observing a couple on a first date that were introduced through a common acquaintance. He starts the conversation by saying, "So, you know so and so?"

She answers in the affirmative and they pass mutual compliments in the direction of the introducing party. He then fills the obligatory small-talk space by asking about how long she has lived in the community, how she likes living there, and what her hobbies are. After a few moments of this patter, he adopts a businesslike demeanor and says: "You know, it's really great to meet you and I look forward to getting to know you better. Just for my information-gathering process, I'm wondering if you would mind giving me a few numbers relevant to this discussion? One, do you have any kids and how old are they? Two, how many people have you dated in the last year? And three, I would guess your measurements to be in the neighborhood of 36-30-42. Am I far off there? By the way, I can see that 42 being a problem, but I have a couple of ideas that might help."

Undoubtedly he would find a drink flying across the table before his spiel had ended!

CURIOSITY'S NATURAL ORDER

As absurd as this example sounds, it is a fair analogy of the artificial and synthetic pattern used in many a financial services conversation. Contemplate for a moment the natural order of conversation.

1. We talk about people and things in common.
2. We often then move into background discovery.
3. We then might do a short survey of present circumstances.
4. We then talk about interests and hopes.

Contrast that naturally occurring order of conversation with the typical pattern found in financial services.

1. We engage in frivolous or superfluous small talk.
2. We start getting the numbers.
3. We point out any problems.
4. We talk about solutions for the future.

Is it any wonder that this conversation pattern often leads to an emotional disconnect on the part of the client? Successful conversations follow the organic path of dialogue: learn some things you don't know about the individual, find out what is important to them, survey their experiences and opinions, and offer suggestions that are in sync with what you have just heard. For this sort of dialogue to be authentic, it must be fueled by 100-octane curiosity.

CURIOSITY'S CHEMICAL REACTION

"All creatures capable of more than a mere mechanical response to stimulus are curious. That is, they explore their world rather than just respond to it," stated Richard Taflinger of Washington State University in a study on curiosity and advertising. He proposed that the biological pressures developing curiosity are immense based on the biological drives of preservation, reproduction, and greed. Taflinger goes on to say, "The greatest advantage of curiosity is the increase in neurological connections it makes possible. Investigating the unusual creates new pathways in the brain. The more pathways, the more possible responses to stimuli, the more possible responses, the greater likelihood of a proper response to another novel situation. Curiosity strengthens these learned responses."

From this study we may conclude that curiosity triggers a number of beneficial reactions in the brain, opening neural pathways toward wisdom and, just as importantly, triggering a sense of empathy between inquirer and respondent.

By following the natural order of conversation, we experience curiosity's chemical reaction, which is triggered in the brain as clients sense that we understand their story and empathize with it. Empathy is sparked by authentic curiosity. A study in 1997 by the American Medical Association found that there were substantially fewer lawsuits by MDs who took the time to purposely display empathy for their clients. Those cynics who might be thinking, "Who has time to display empathy with everything else I need to cover in these meetings?" might be interested in knowing how long it took these liability-insulated physicians to display empathy—on average, 90 seconds!

PUTTING THE QUEST BACK INTO THE QUESTION

Knowing what we do about questions, curiosity, empathy, and their ameliorative impact on client relationships, we would suggest that the time has come to put the "quest" back into question. Every question you ask should be well thought out, purposeful, and useful toward the larger context of building empathy and a lasting relationship with your clients. Discard the throwaway questions and begin assembling those questions that will give you useful knowledge and enable your biographical intentions.

How much do you know about your most treasured or most desired clients? Do you know where they are from and what life was like for them back there? Do you know about their family growing up? Do you know about their educational and career paths? Do you understand the greatest challenges, concerns, and obstacles in their lives at the present time? In the chapter that follows, we will demonstrate a model for adding depth and substance to your inquiry process and a way for you to blend the quantitative and the qualitative aspects of your clients' situations so powerfully that your clients would never dream of leaving you for another provider.

You will rarely, if ever, experience clients pulling away when you are exercising genuine curiosity. Clients pull away when they feel control pulling at them. At that point resistance embraces resolve. As you anticipate this new conversation, let us challenge you with a new conversational goal: to make fewer statements, ask better questions, and remain cognitive at all times of your own impulses and training toward trying to "control the conversation." Let it go and see where curiosity takes you.

6

MERGING THE QUANTITATIVE AND THE QUALITATIVE

An Introduction to Financial Life Planning

"You've got a 200-piece jigsaw puzzle lying on the table in front of you. What is the first and most important piece? Most people will say the corner piece, but the answer is the picture on the cover of the box."

Elizabeth Jetton, CFP, past president of the Financial Planning Association

Most advisors are gathering a story of numbers from their clients when what they ought to be gathering is a number of stories.

A financial advisor from New Jersey recently told us a story that poignantly illustrates the need to ask the right questions. He told us about attending a big meeting with a client and his attorney and accountant. The advisor quickly became frustrated in this meeting because the attorney had taken complete control of the meeting. It was as if the attorney was the quarterback and everyone else was just running their routes on the plays he called for the client. The advisor told us that he didn't necessarily disagree with the attorney's direction but found himself in a secondary or maybe even tertiary role—and wondered why it was this way.

The advisor decided to listen closely to the questions the attorney was asking the client and compare them with the questions he had been asking when suddenly the coin dropped for him. He realized that he had been asking what, where, and how questions.

"What do you have, where is it, and how should we manage it?" The lawyer, on the other hand, was asking the big-picture questions, such as "Who is this for, and why do you want to do this?" His questions were setting up the context for everything the others were doing.

The advisor told us that it was then that he realized that the "quarterback" in every client scenario is the person asking the better questions. From that day forward he decided to make sure that he was the one asking the important questions.

Perhaps you don't like the position in which you find yourself in some of your client relationships. It might be time to begin studying the game films of successful quarterbacks in this industry. The best in the business know how to ask questions that cut to the heart of what matters most to the client.

THE REAL EFFECT OF NUMBERS

How do you feel about sitting down and filling out loan applications? Financial forms? Applications of any sort? It is a mundane, repetitious, dreary process that most people would bypass if they could. Below the superficial task of filling out the forms lie the emotional objections of revealing private information, being defined by numbers, and the possibility of not being considered important enough.

How easily we slip into defining our relationships by numbers: "I just saw my million-dollar client," or "I just landed a half-million-dollar client." How do you suppose your clients would feel knowing they were being described this way?

Part of the research for this book involved looking at the information-gathering forms used by many of the major financial firms in the industry. What we found is best characterized by Scott's comment, "It's like participating in a Bataan death march of numbers." How sad that this industry has reduced the rewarding art of curiosity to sterile number-gathering exercises like fact finding, financial disclosure, and risk assessment. Seen in this light, the oft-used term *client profiling* doesn't have the right ring to it, does it? Scott has often said that his favorite description of this process is the "probing sequence." He says, "I don't know about you but I don't want to go to a financial advisor and get probed anytime soon."

Mitch once received a call from a firm to critique their redesigned discovery forms. They sent their forms to Mitch on Friday and scheduled a conference call for Monday morning.

In reviewing the forms, Mitch found approximately 100 questions—95 of which were quantitative in nature. What do you have? How much? How long? Where is it? What are your account numbers? The first question that could be characterized as qualitative was Which of the following is your goal?, and gave options such as putting a child through college, retirement, buying a second home, etc.

When the Monday morning call came, Mitch informed them of their ratio of quantitative and qualitative inquiry, and then complimented them on their sociological research or clairvoyance—or whatever it was that enabled them to reduce every American's goals to a list of five. He also shared with them the emotional fact that the imbalance of quantitative inquiry in the process made him feel "like a safe-deposit box to which you are trying to find the combination."

And these inquiry forms were the new and improved versions that this firm was using! We can't imagine how much fun the client had with the previous version. To be fair, we will concede that statistical information is important; however, our assertion is that it is peripheral in importance when compared to the qualitative information that defines the context of who the client is and what is important to him or her.

SHORTCHANGED BY NUMBERS

We wouldn't begin a client interview by asking, "How are you, and how much do you have?" Neither should we progress into numbers gathering until the proper emotional context has been established for the work we will do.

There is only so much that the numbers can tell. They speak only to the material side of the equation. When the popular physicist, Brian Greene, was asked why he was such a good communicator (unlike his peers) he said, "I don't feel like I understand what I'm doing unless I can form a mental picture of what's going on. If I'm relying on mathematical symbols, I feel like I've got the true heart of the science. When it comes to communicating with the public, I take those mental pictures I've developed, strip away the math, and wrap them in a story."

The true science of financial advice is in the story the client tells.

There is a story to be told about every number you gather and, in many cases, a very important story. We once heard an accountant give a presentation about the fact that he one day realized that there was an important story behind every fact and number on a 1040 tax form. Those who harvest those stories will be in better stead with the client because, in the client's mind, the number is not nearly as important as the work and love and sacrifice that produced it.

Numbers and facts tell us what clients have. They do not tell us how hard they worked, what they had to sacrifice, who has and will benefit, who inspired the dream, the hardships they overcame, the pain and joy they experienced in the journey, partnerships formed and broken, and the amazing breaks and bad fortune navigated in gathering the assets those numbers represent. Behind every success story is a genealogy of events and relationships— one leading into the other—that come together to form incredibly unique biographies. Your job, first and foremost, and in respect to the price each client has paid, is to uncover as much of that biographical genealogy as possible.

This work is performed best by curious individuals—not by printed applications.

TO THE HEART OF THE MATTER

So often our discovery work fails to get to the heart of what is really important to the client and what their money really represents. Believing in the importance of a disciplined and repeatable discovery process that focuses on the financial matters arising out of the *life* of the client, the Financial Life Planning Institute developed the chart in Figure 6.1. This chart illustrates the difference between quantitative and qualitative inquiry, and the sort of discovery that is most important to the client.

The efforts of the financial services industry are concentrated in the various aspects of financial planning in the outer circle: asset management, taxes, debt/cash flow planning, risk management, distribution planning, and estate planning. The approaches to these facets of financial planning are largely quantitative in nature and often fail to grasp the larger context in the client's life; namely, this is about me, not just my money. *The client's quality of life* is in line with the decisions we are making here. This is the heart of the matter.

We have discovered that the industry has done a tidy job of creating structured methodologies for obtaining quantitative information from clients, processing that information, and then spitting that information back in a report or plan. But when it comes to qualitative information—the experiences, principles, and deepest hopes and fears of their clients—these matters are too often left to whim or chance.

The quantitative aspects of discovery in the chart in Figure 6.1 illustrate the *dialogue path* necessary for truly understanding a

FIGURE 6.1 *Financial Life Planning Wheel*

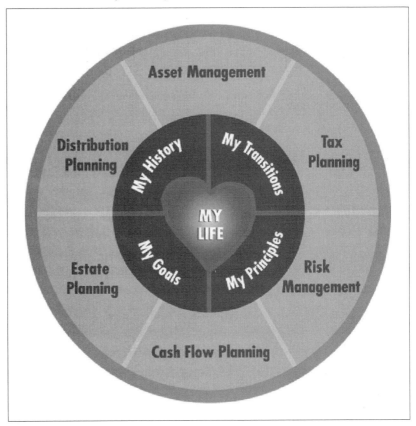

© 2004 Mitch Anthony

client and for most effectively delivering financial solutions. The best news of all is that this is not a new process you need to learn. It's natural! It's the way we have built the most satisfying relationships we hold dear in our lives. It's the natural order of curiosity. This path for quantitative discovery is:

- History (where I've been)
- Transitions (where I am now)
- Principles (how I got here)
- Goals (where I'd like to go)

In our research on the quantitative inquiry being conducted in the financial services industry, we have found that most financial professionals focus on *client goals*. By and large, this focus on goals is premature and problematic. Goals should actually be the last arena we delve into, in terms of quantitative inquiry. Inquiry into a client's history, current transitions, and underlying principles should logically precede the goals inquiry.

Why? How often have you seen clients who will never reach their goals because of the patterns and habits they have formed with money? This awareness arises in the history inquiry. How often have you seen clients whose lives are filled with so many issues impeding their financial progress that their goals will never materialize? We see it all the time. We are not saying that goals discovery is unimportant, but rather, that in the context of knowing our clients, it should be the "caboose" in the conversation and not the "engine."

To really know our clients we need to know their past, and their past with money. We also need to have a comprehensive knowledge of their present life circumstances and challenges. This is where your greatest opportunities lie. How can we claim to know any of our clients if we cannot articulate their most important principles and philosophies regarding money and investing?

Mitch has been challenging advisors who claim to know their clients well to write down the names of their top ten clients and then write down the top two or three matters or concerns in those clients' lives right now. Very few have ever been able to complete the exercise. Why? Until recently, the tools for this type of discovery have been nonexistent. In this book we will begin to introduce some of the groundbreaking tools developed by the Financial Life Planning Institute for discovering the life of your client. These tools are revolutionizing the way many firms and advisors practice and are helping to redefine the advisor-client relationship.

In Part II of this book, we will take a tour down this suggested dialogue path of history, transitions, principles, and goals, and then introduce the questions you can ask, resources you can use, and dialogues you can expect. Before we get too far down the quantitative dialogue path, we need to address a bigger-picture issue: *How do you begin this conversation?*

OPENING THE BROADER CONVERSATION

We believe that the first five to ten minutes of a client conversation should be spent on establishing the context of your services and the role you want to play in the client's life. Following are some conversational openers and approaches we have found to be helpful in establishing this all-important context.

Important Pieces

It has been well said that "context is worth 50 IQ points" and nowhere is that more true than in the dialogue between the advisor and client. When we speak of the "bigger picture" we are really referring to *context*. Contextual curiosity housed in the right side of your client's brain longs to know, "What are you going to do to fit in with the larger context of my life and my goals?" When the right side of the brain sees a shard, it wants to know what the entire relic looks like. When it hears beautiful lyrics, it wants to know the story behind them. This is context. This is the bigger picture that smart communicators address up front because they know that once the audience understands the context, they pay more attention to everything that follows.

Are you speaking to this larger context in your client presentations or are you majoring on specifics and individual pieces? As the quote by Elizabeth Jetton at the beginning of this chapter suggests, the client needs to know how your services fit into the big picture. This industry has been doing little else than simply "moving pieces" of the puzzle around on the table for far too long. For example, "What rate of return are you getting over there? Let me move that over here." Or, "How much are you paying for that? Let me move that piece over here as well."

Someone—and it might as well be you—needs to step up and address the larger context of the purposes and grand design this money will address. How do you introduce the larger context into your conversations with clients? One advisor asks his clients to send in a family picture before their scheduled meeting. He takes the photo to a local printing shop that converts the family picture into a small jigsaw puzzle. He uses the jigsaw puzzle with their picture to open his conversation.

If you think that sounds a little corny, you might consider the fact that this advisor manages over $900 million dollars for his clients. Maybe his understanding of establishing context in the heart of the client has something to do with his success.

The Means or the End?

We met a successful financial planner who begins his meeting by asking, "Is money a means or an end for you?" He says that 99 percent of the people will respond that money is a means—to which he answers, "If money is a means, then before I make any suggestions as to how that money be invested or managed, I need to know to what end. Would you mind if I took some time to learn more about the people and things in your life?" From there the conversation moves into matters that are meaningful to the client. This planner has now established a relevant and emotional context for his service. For the other 1 percent that answers that money is the end, he offers the caveat that you may want to question whether or not you really want those clients because they can be difficult to please.

What Is Important to You?

Bill Bachrach, author of *Values-Based Selling*, teaches the contextual setup of asking, "What is important about money to you?" If a client says it is freedom, the Bachrach method teaches to ask, "What is important about freedom to you?" If the client answers, "Being able to do what I want with my time," Bachrach recommends following up with, "What is important about being able to do what you want with your time?" and so on and so forth.

While the advisor jury is split on the comfort level of delivering this sort of repetitive questioning path, many like the fact that it opens a larger, more emotionally based context for the services they will perform.

FINANCIAL LIFE CHECKUP

Advisors who work with the Financial Life Planning Institute utilize a tool called the "Financial Life Checkup" (see Figure 6.2) as a context-setting and service-defining tool with their clients and prospects. This tool was designed in response to research that found that *the more money people make in America the less they sleep*. The Financial Life Planning Institute concluded that Americans were not getting their money's worth from their paycheck in terms of satisfaction and designed this instrument for clients to rate their level of satisfaction with over 20 aspects of their financial life. After all, from the clients' point of view, it's not how much money we have, but how much payoff we receive from that money in terms of our quality of life. The areas of inquiry included in the Financial Life Checkup include: cash-flow management, risk management, investments and benefit programs, personal financial management, personal financial education, estate management, and qualitative questions that query the areas of finance management that rob them of satisfaction and peace of mind.

FIGURE 6.2 *Financial Life Checkup*

Satisfaction Level

Least					Most
1	2	3	4		5

Cash Flow Management
1. My ability to meet my financial obligations _____
2. The income my current job or career provides me _____
3. My spending habits _____
4. The spending habits of my family members _____
5. Managing my debt _____
6. Managing to maintain an adequate emergency fund _____

Risk Management / Investments / Benefits
7. The amount and types of insurance protection I currently have _____
8. My ability to protect my current cash flow _____
9. The amount of money that I save and invest on a regular basis _____
10. My ability to meet short-term financial goals _____
11. My ability to meet my long-term financial goals under my current financial plan (education, retirement, etc.) _____
12. The level of employee benefits I receive _____

Management / Estate / Education
13. My personal financial recordkeeping and management _____
14. My ability to manage my financial plan _____
15. My plan for protection/transfer of my assets _____
16. My income/estate tax reduction strategy _____
17. My level of charitable giving _____
18. My current level of financial education _____

Qualitative Issues
19. How I respond or react to difficult financial circumstances _____
20. My ability to maintain my current lifestyle (cash flow) _____
21. My ability and willingness to communicate about finances _____
22. The level of meaning my finances bring to my life _____
23. How my finances affect my personal relationships _____
24. The overall relationship I have with my financial advisor _____

© 2004 Mitch Anthony

From this survey advisors are then able to generate a personalized report (see Figure 6.3) for each client based on their answers. This personalized report becomes the context-setting discussion piece as advisors walk through each client's areas of high, medium, and low degrees of satisfaction in their initial meeting. Advisors inform their clients that they view their mission to be helping them realize more satisfaction for their money so they can enjoy it more and worry about it less. This establishes the emotional context that every client hungers for, regardless of their income level.

DEVELOPING BIOGRAPHIES

Once you have established the proper context—your client's hopes, dreams, and life satisfaction—you are now prepared to play the role of biographer. You say to your client, "In order for me to do a good job and to tailor my services to you and your life, I'm going to ask a few questions about you, the people important to you, and the things going on in your life. Is that OK with you?" If this client or prospect responds to this invitation to dialogue by saying, "No, I just want to buy a bond fund," then, help them find the best bond fund possible. Our experience, however, shows that most people are not only willing to engage in this sort of financial life dialogue but hunger to do so.

You are now ready to begin the financial life dialogue that discovers your client's history, transitions, principles, and goals. You may conduct this biographical in a session or two, or just collect pieces of their story over time. Two objections we often hear from advisors at this point are:

1. I don't have time for this.
2. What do I say to clients that I've had for years but never made this sort of inquiry with before?

FIGURE 6.3 *Financial Life Checkup Personal Report*

Financial Life Checkup Summary

Joe Client, 2/7/2005

Area of Examination	Satisfaction Level
Areas that need immediate attention (Satisfaction Levels of 1 or 2)	
The income my current job or career provides me	1
My income/estate tax reduction strategy	2
My ability to meet financial obligations	2
My ability to protect my current cash flow	2
Areas that need further diagnosis (Satisfaction Level of 3)	
How I respond or react to difficult financial circumstances	3
The amount and types of insurance protection I currently have	3
My level of charitable giving	3
The amount of money that I save and invest on a regular basis	3
My plan for protection/transfer of my assets	3
My spending habits of family members	3
The level and quality of employee benefits I receive	3
Areas that appear to be in good financial health (Satisfaction Levels of 4 or 5)	
Managing to maintain an adequate emergency fund	4
My current level of financial education	4
My ability to meet short-term financial goals	4
My ability to meet long-term financial goals under my current financial plan (education, retirement, etc.)	4
My ability to maintain my current lifestyle (cash flow)	4
How my finances affect my personal relationships	4
The level of meaning that I receive from my finances	4
My ability and willingness to communicate about finances	4
My personal financial recordkeeping and management	4
My ability to manage my financial plan	4
The level of satisfaction I have with my financial professionals	4
Managing my debt	5
My spending habits	5

The time issue is a myth. You have time. Take a close look at your present conversations with clients. You are simply trading small talk and market-speak for meaningful qualitative dialogue. Scott has been conducting an experiment in the last year that addresses this time concern. He allows advisors exactly 38 minutes to learn as much as they can about each other's history, transitions, principles, and goals. The results are amazing and myth-exploding.

Scott's findings in his "Speed Meeting" Workshop (a 24-minute get-to-know-you exercise utilizing the natural order of curiosity) implode most theories of what it takes to get to know people. When participants leave the meeting they are shaking hands. There are significant bonds being born in exercises lasting only minutes but focused on genuine curiosity. Participants noted that in this 24-minute time frame, the relationship moved from the factual to familiar and, in some cases, toward real friendships. One advisor noted that he went through this exercise after having spent five hours with the same individual at a football game and dinner the day before. "I learned more about this guy in a few minutes with the right questions than I did all last night being together." If you are intent on knowing your clients, you can go miles in minutes with properly designed questions.

If you have never made such qualitative inquiry into the lives of your clients, you need not be embarrassed. You can casually segue into a more meaningful conversation by saying something like, "I was thinking as I was preparing for you to come in today about the fact that I don't know if I ever asked you where you grew up and where you went to school. You know life changes so fast for all of us. To make sure I'm up to date on all that's happening in your life, let me ask you, 'Is there anything else in your personal or professional life that might be affecting your financial life?'" Most people can't resist the opportunity to talk about their story—and you are now making a more meaningful connection to their life.

WHY THE "WHY" AND WHY THE "WHO"?

How many people are informed enough about your life to see past *what* you do to *why* you do it? How many people are informed enough of your material life to see past what you have to how you achieved it and what you really want out of it? How many people are informed enough about your life to see past your profession and job title and know what really motivates you in work and in life? The people that know these things about us fall into two categories: those who have grown up with us or those who have taken the time to learn it.

As an advisor, the latter path is your best opportunity. There are only so many people we know that well as a result of our family and environment. You will find that your sincere inquiry into the qualitative aspects of your clients' and prospective clients' lives will produce more than income—it will produce lasting relationships and friendships.

And it will produce clients for life.

7

WHERE YOUR CLIENT HAS BEEN

Mastering the Historical Inquiry

"The past is prologue."

William Shakespeare

"Tell me a fact and I'll learn,
Tell me a truth and I'll believe,
Tell me a story and it will live in my heart forever."

Steve Sabol, NFL Films

In December of 2001, the market was down and so were my clients. This was three months after 9/11 and I wanted to talk to my clients, and, of course, they wanted to talk with me.

Beginning early on the day of December 6, I called each client who was 75 and older. The question I asked each person was exactly the same: 'Mr./Mrs._____, I am calling you to find out how this life-changing event affected you, and what changes it caused in your life. I want you to know that the sacrifice you and your generation made is appreciated by me and my generation.' Then I thanked each of my clients for telling me their stories and thanked them for being clients of mine.

These calls were quite emotional in some cases, and the market went down that day—all day—but it was the best day I ever had with clients.

Each of my clients knew exactly what had happened to their lives on December 7, 1941—and now I know as well.
Wallace Zealy, financial advisor

We are convinced, chronologically speaking, that the common approach to qualitative discovery is misguided. We believe one of the reasons advisors gather only 30 percent to 40 percent of their clients' assets is that their premature questioning about their clients' future is at best presumptive and in no way affords the right to full disclosure. Most models encourage advisors to talk about goals with clients, for example, "Where would you like to be in five years?" when a much richer conversation could have been prompted with, "Tell me where you've been in the last five years."

The past is known——the future is unknown. Do you want to begin trying to build relationships on the vague and the formless or is it better to begin building on the known, the experienced, and the objective, complete with lessons learned? We advise the latter.

Once your eyes are open to the importance of the history inquiry, you will find yourself developing an insatiable appetite for knowing people's stories because you understand that these stories explain almost everything: who they really are, how they grew up, how their life has evolved, how they have built the life they have. Talk about knowing your customer! How much of this information do you currently know about your clients? How much better would your clients be if you did know these defining stories? You might be pleasantly surprised as you pursue the history inquiry.

We would go so far to say that the future of your relationship with each of your clients hinges on how much you know about their past.

Your first and most important task is to act as biographer. As Wallace described above, your relationships and your job take on a new richness, a fresh significance when you understand an important piece of history from each client's life.

The past *is* prologue. You cannot possibly begin to understand the essence of the person sitting before you without knowing their context—that context in *his*-story or *her*-story, as the case may be.

So, exactly what stories do we want to hear? What pieces of information are most important to gather as a financial biographer? Maybe we shouldn't be asking about what information you are gathering but which associations, in your client's mind, you are aware of. We have been misguided about how the mind works and this misguidance has guided the design of our discovery processes. The mind doesn't naturally operate on a logic-seeking or information-filing sequence but rather on an association mechanism known as a synapse. Brain science estimates that the number of possible associations our brain is capable of is the number six followed by 10,000 miles of zeros!

When you bring up an idea or thought with clients, their mind immediately seeks out links to other experiences, observations, memories, and associations that your idea provokes in the synapse system. What are those associations? This is what we really need to know.

As we mentioned in Chapter 6, when physicist Brian Greene was asked why he was so much better than his peers at communicating, he answered: "If I'm relying on mathematical symbols, I don't feel like I have the true heart of the science. When it comes to communicating with the public, I take those mental pictures I've developed, strip away the math, and wrap them in a story."

In financial services, the true science of what you do is not found in the math but in the stories you evoke from clients.

Although there are many attractive and interesting trails to take as you stroll down memory lane with clients, there are three sites you want to be sure not to miss. They are:

1. Important (defining) events in their life
2. Recollections around money
3. Past experiences with money

Following we will introduce questions you can build into your inquiry to gain a richer understanding of your clients' history. By engaging in these dialogues you will better understand the events and environment that shaped them, the defining aspects of their life, and their experiences with money.

RECOLLECTIONS AROUND MONEY

One of our favorite maxims is: No matter how high the branch grows or how fruitful it becomes, it is never removed from its roots.

Here are five questions you can ask:

1. What is your first memory around money?
2. What was your first job?
3. What kind of work did your parents do?
4. What events have happened in your life that you would describe as defining moments?
5. Looking back, what is the time in your life where you were most satisfied with your money situation?

The beauty of the history dialogue is that participants are thankful for both the personal awareness and disclosure it allows, and also knowing that you, their advisor, understand what they're all about. There is so little we can know about our clients from their name, age, profession, job title, and net worth. A short dialogue about their personal history, however, can reveal reams of information that forms cannot.

In the process of articulating their story, you will begin to see powerful emotional "souvenirs." These include reminders of:

- Humble beginnings (Look from what and where I came)
- Pride of achievement (Look at what I've accomplished)
- Lessons learned (I've grown along the way)

Question 1: What is your first memory about money? This question has led to some of the most remarkable and meaningful conversations with clients. Mitch was on an airplane and fell into a discussion with the gentleman next to him who mentioned that he was the CEO of a publicly traded manufacturing firm. Mitch mentioned that he developed "dialogues around money." Interested, the man asked for an example, so Mitch asked him about his first memory around money.

The man's eyes almost glazed over as he took himself back to his childhood and said, "I'm sitting on a couch in Cleveland, and the couch . . . is . . . on the street corner. We've been evicted for the third time. My friends and neighbors are driving by and gawking and I'm so embarrassed. My dad washes windows 12 to 14 hours a day but can't support his 11 children."

Mitch explored more of the story, asking about this man's father's business and struggles, and the ramifications for this man in his own professional and financial life. Mitch then asked him if he had a financial advisor, and he said he did. Mitch asked if his financial planner knew this important story from his past. The man raised his eyebrow and said, "Come to think of it he's never asked about my past."

We need not ask the obvious here, do we?

If you were his financial planner would you *want* to know this story? We would go so far as to say that you probably couldn't hit the bull's-eye in meeting this client's agenda without knowing this story. The past is prologue. You couldn't possibly know this client without knowing his story.

Question 2: What was your first job? or, What kind of work did you do as a kid? One individual, when asked this question, shared the story of how, at the age of ten, he began selling Christmas trees door-to-door. The idea then struck him that he might be able to follow up with Christmas accessories and later with Christmas cards. His business was humming along every holiday season until he ran into inventory problems—his supplier couldn't keep up with him!

Others will talk about the paper route, dishwashing, or table-waiting jobs. People that grew up in rural settings will talk about getting up at 5:00 AM to do chores. Others will talk about helping out in the family business or mowing lawns. No matter what their stories are, you will gain valuable insight from listening to their stories. If they didn't work as a kid, there is an insight there as well. In the story above, we learned that this young entrepreneur had a mind for business at a young age and understood inefficiency in business when he saw it. This would be helpful background information if you planned on taking this individual as a client.

This recollection seems to be a favorite for people as it allows them to review their early resume and the humble beginnings from which they may have sprouted.

Question 3: What kind of work did your parents do? "My Dad was a teacher and my mother was a homemaker and somehow they supported and fed 12 children," Pat began. "And to this day I don't have a clue how they held it all together. I have the ultimate respect for my parents for what they did and how little they had to work with. Try to imagine raising 12 children today on a teacher's salary."

The question of how their family earned a living leads into the economic periphery of your clients' lives. No matter how financially successful your clients may be, their central identity is tied more to their generating circumstances than to their present circumstances. People are emotionally anchored to the economic experiences they had growing up.

In this history dialogue people will often volunteer their formative economic stratum that they grew up "poor" or "decidedly middle-class" or "pretty comfortable." They almost always have stories to tell about their parents. You don't need us to tell you that these stories are most important for understanding the fabric out of which your client's values around money were cut.

"My father was a radio journalist," Andy volunteered. "He supported a family of seven on what I later realized was a very thin budget. But I understood my dad's resourcefulness by the fact that he and his mother were abandoned by his father and early on he had to fend for himself—as well as contribute to the family coffers. He passed that on to all of his children, requiring us to earn our spending money as soon as we could find a way to make a buck. And I am now teaching my kids the same way."

This economic genealogy very often flows naturally into how their parents grew up as well to complete the portrait of their economic molding. These stories are invaluable for grasping each individual client's values, structures, and expectations around money. Think of your own economic history, upbringing, and humble beginnings and how these experiences have shaped you as a person and you will then have the proper image of what it means to "know your client."

Question 4: What events have happened in your life that you would describe as defining moments? Until you have the discovered the answer to this question, we would suggest that you have not found your way to the core of what deeply motivates your client. For example, the defining moment in Gene's life came when he was a young man. A fire burned down his parents' house, swallowed their most valued possessions, and threw their lives into temporary chaos and turmoil. As you hear Gene describe this event, you realize that it not only changed his parents' lives but his professional/career track as well. As a result of the incident, he decided that life was too short and unpredictable and that he would stay near his parents to earn his living.

The following examples are stories that came to light after asking this question, indicating not only the attitude each client has toward money, but also how they came to be who they are. Think through the ramifications of the following scenarios.

- Anne's husband died on their honeymoon after a drunk driver hit them.
- Wilson described his parents' divorce. He depicted the surviving familial stresses and the economic struggles encountered by both parents.
- Sophia talked of her father losing his job as an air traffic controller during the showdown with the Reagan presidency and the challenges it presented to her father's career and her family's well-being.
- Doug talked of his father losing the family farm during the farm crisis in the Midwest in the early 1980s. His father started driving a truck and the family moved into town.

This question is a bit of a double-edged sword. If you ask the question, be prepared to hear some profound and moving stories. If you don't ask, you will never know what it is you don't know about this individual. Not all the stories are about grief, loss, and pain. Some of the defining moments in people's lives are about windfalls, success stories, and good fortune. Other stories are an amalgam of good and bad.

- Tony's father inherited land from his father, which turned out to be in the path of their city's expansion. Tony's father received an amazing price for the land and the windfall was a life-changing event for the entire family. They moved to a new home, the children attended a new school, and the family went on trips they could never before afford—and saw a more relaxed father.
- Maya's mother had decided to return to the classroom and attend law school at night. This had a short-term impact on their living arrangements but led to a long-term rise in their standard of living and in their mother's dependence on an undependable ex-husband's support.

- Will was out having beers one night with his teammates after a softball game when one of them proposed a business idea. The four of them agreed that it was worth a try. Two years later, Will was the beneficiary of a multimillion-dollar buyout.
- Jon escaped the harpoon of a communist officer as he jumped off a boat and swam to freedom's shore leaving his family and home behind in Romania. A harpoon killed his partner in the escape. Grateful for America's freedom and rewards of industriousness, he developed a large landscaping business in a thriving community.

The significant event the client speaks of may be an isolated event or may be a significant period of history that he or she lived through. A case in point is the mature individual who has plenty of assets but spends as if poverty is just around the next corner because he grew up in the Great Depression. Whether it be a traumatic event, a change in fortune, a loss, or a survival story set against the backdrop of history, these stories are shaping your clients' lives like the sculptor's chisel to the stone he carves—leaving irreversible, indelible marks that define who they are and what they become. Few stories can be heard that are as important, in terms of building relationships, as these stories.

DAYS OF MILK AND HONEY

Question 5: Looking back, what is the time in your life where you were most satisfied with your money situation? It is ironic to note that financial satisfaction and a person's highest earnings do not necessarily correspond. If you were to survey a number of people and ask them about the time in their lives they had the most money as well as the time period they were the happiest, they might end up talking about two different times and places. Here are some stories we have heard over the years.

- A young woman in her early 20s, married with a young child, shared about living in a small ranch-style house with a house payment of $150 dollars a month. She was making about $2,000 a month, but her cost of living (food, insurance, car payment, utilities, everything) was under $1,000. She told about selling a car that she had purchased while in college. She put the proceeds (just over $1,700) in the bank and felt like Thurston Howell, III, from *Gilligan's Island*. She had money in the bank, very little debt, and was making twice as much as she needed to survive!"

- A young man shared about his college years. He was working part time and supplementing the rest of his college expenses with a partial scholarship and student loans. Reminiscing, he shared how he was a master chef of ramen noodles, macaroni and cheese, and other fine pastas. He had a car that he had purchased for $200 and it ran great. Ironically, there had never been a time in his life that he had so little, but was so content. It was about survival then—and he was managing quite well. As the years went by, life became more complicated, and it became harder to separate survival from consumerism.

- A couple shared how badly they wanted to start a family but they were afraid and hesitant because of their credit card situation and spending habits. They sat down one night and set a goal to trim certain luxuries and excesses out of their budget, pay off all credit cards within a year, look for other ways to lower their cost of living (like sell the foreign luxury car they had no need for) so that the wife could quit working and be a stay-at-home mom for at least four years. They remember the best moment of their lives was the day they learned the gender of their baby (a girl) and got their first zeroed-out credit card statement. It was on the same day and they were jazzed! That day they took a scissors to that card and never looked back.

- One man shared about the mixed blessing of receiving an inheritance from his father. He was finally able to retire and pursue some of the things he had always dreamed of doing. Although he sorely misses his father, he gets to wake up every day and know that he has his life back—a reminder of his father and what his hard work years ago has done for him.

These conversations can help people sort out the relationship between money and contentment—and bring awareness of the fact that money does not always guarantee contentment. Our relationship to debt, our spending habits, our susceptibility to making whimsical purchases, and the hours we have to work all work in concert with our income to deliver the much desired contentment that we are chasing. This is a conversation that can easily lead to debt and risk management, as well as tax and estate planning. It can help people define what financial contentment looks like, help them expedite the path to that place, and help ensure that they can make it their permanent address. That's what this conversation is all about.

In the next chapter we will delve into a different sort of history conversation about your clients' experiences with financial products, services, and financial service providers. Our thesis around the history inquiry is this: the path to your future relationship with your clients runs through their past. Every ounce of energy you expend in the history inquiry will be measured back to you in pounds in terms of the quality of the relationship.

8

THE EXPERIENCE INQUIRY

Gaining Perspective through Your Clients'
Experiences with Money and Financial Services

"The successful companies of the 21st century will be the ones satisfying
emotional needs."

Rolf Jensen, *The Dream Society*

CLIENTS DIVING UNDER TABLES

In the movie *The Big Lebowski,* John Goodman plays a Vietnam vet with a serious case of post-traumatic stress syndrome (PTSS) who, being quickly triggered to the edge of his rage, continually states, "You don't know where I've been, man!" He wanted people to respect what he'd been through before they started making suggestions for him.

While we're not suggesting that your average client or prospect is in danger of losing it, we are suggesting that, emotional speaking, this is an area of inquiry you want to engage in *before* you decide to take on a client. We also feel quite safe in saying, via mass client diagnosis, that there is no shortage of Post-Traumatic Investment Syndrome (PTIS) out there, and you'll want to keep your radar up. The best solution to PTIS is to be proactive.

PTIS proliferated with the confluence of events that heralded the beginning of this millennium: the dot-com bubble of 2000,

9/11, and the never-ending revelations of corporate corruption—specifically, in the financial services sector.

There is a good chance that almost every person you meet has had a regrettable experience with either their money and/or with a provider of financial services. If you begin to talk about your products and services before conducting what we like to refer to as *the land mine sweep,* you are putting yourself in peril's path.

Unwittingly, you can use certain language, a certain tone, or suggest a product or idea that has been the source for a regrettable experience in the client's past. While it's not your fault for sounding like something or someone else, you are culpable for the fact that you took your prospect by the arm and went square dancing into that emotional minefield without first doing your reconnaissance.

Clients may not say anything to indicate that you said something that bothered them. They may just check out with their body language and tell you they just want to "think about it."

All you have to do is ask.

Mitch accompanied his mother to her initial visit with a financial advisor. They had talked to a number of advisors but this particular one was the first to explore her past experiences with the question, "Have you had any experiences with other financial services providers that you would like to tell me about?"

For a few seconds you could have heard a pin drop. Then Mitch's mother unraveled the story of how a so-called "friend" in the insurance business had advised her to put the majority of her inheritance into an annuity with severe restrictions and penalties and had suggested an allocation that later proved disastrous. Adding insult to injury, this "friend" no longer returned her phone calls.

The advisor who asked was glad that he did, and so was Mitch! Mitch's mother was noticeably impressed with the inquiry and felt a sense of relief in telling the story to this advisor. It was her opportunity to let him know where she had been. There was certainly a case of PTIS to be dealt with here and he handled the situation by educating her on all the nuances and fine print you need to know about annuities.

Clients or prospects may be wrong in their interpretation or assessment of the situation, but you are still better off being aware of their views in these matters lest you wander down a path that triggers a sabotaging synapse. You don't want to say something or recommend a product that sends the client diving under the conference table.

The wisest advisors we know do a clean sweep of this potential minefield in the client's memory before they proceed to their own recommendations. Those who fail to perform this "sweep" of principles are indeed taking their prospects and clients out for a square dance in a minefield and will at best come away limping, or end up DOA in a worst-case scenario.

Our recommendation, as throughout all client discovery procedures, is to find out where they've been before you bother finding out where they want to go. Knowing the path that led them to this place only raises the odds that you'll partner with them on the path that leads them away from this place. This is especially true as it pertains to the financial experiences dialogue.

SEEING THE MONEY DOCTOR

Can you remember how the conversation started the first time you visited a new doctor? Chances are that the physician's interview contained numerous questions about your personal health and your family's history with certain conditions. This brings to mind two questions that are allegorical to the financial services industry and much needed in your interviews with prospects:

1. Are you seeing any other physicians? If so, what have they told you?
2. Do you have any known allergies to medicine?

What other advisors are your prospects seeing, and what sort of advice are they getting from these individuals? Is this something you want to know? It is if you plan on being a 100 percent advisor who helps people design a financial plan for each aspect and transition in life. Are they here for a second opinion or because they are not happy with the treatment or results they have been getting? It will help you to know the experiential premise for this prospect showing up in your office.

Prospects and clients potentially have allergies to every imaginable product or service you could possibly offer. The allergy has little to do with the nature of the product or service but everything to do with their *reaction* to that product or service. They have a reaction because of something that happened to them or to a friend or family member, or it may be because of something they read or heard. You won't necessarily see their eyes start watering or their skin break out in hives or their loud fits of sneezing because the reaction is happening inside their emotional memory. In fact, the physical response of a financial allergy may be complete atrophy or a freezing up of responses.

An advisor told us about presenting what he thought would be a very good annuity solution for an older client. The client didn't remark or respond during the entire explanation although the advisor told us he did a very good job of delivering it.

When the advisor finished his presentation, the older gentleman looked him in the eye and simply said, "Nope."

The advisor asked, "Why do you feel that way about annuities?"

The man remarked, "I saw a special on them on *60 Minutes* and I don't want anything to do with them!"

End of conversation.

Our thought on the preceding anecdote is that maybe you ought to determine the client's feelings about financial products and services *before* you present an idea or solution. Why not check for allergies before rubbing hay in the client's face? We will now present the inquiries we have compiled regarding:

- Your client's experiences with other providers
- Your client's financial history
- Your client's expectations of you as an advisor
- Gaining feedback on your practice

OTHER PEOPLE'S PRACTICES

Have you had any experiences with other financial service providers (good or bad) that you might want to tell me about?

This question will open the door not only to the potential emotional land mines in your clients' financial lives but will also give you an idea of the other professionals they are interacting with and the sophistication level of their expectations. If someone has been neglected, you'll hear about it in this conversation. If they were charged too much or put in an inappropriate product, this will surface as well. Here are the sorts of answers you may hear when asking this question.

- "We had a really good advisor, but he left the business for personal health reasons. Then the company transferred our accounts to someone we really didn't care for." (This response could open an inquiry into both why they appreciated the advisor they lost and how the new advisor had erred in connecting with them. This is a pretty good foundation for beginning an advisor-client relationship, wouldn't you say?)
- "In 1999, I let an advisor talk me into buying a large amount of telecommunications stocks with money I really couldn't afford to lose. After they had lost 50 percent of their value, he called me back—I hadn't heard from him in the interim—and basically talked me into 'doubling down' on these stocks—I think he called it 'cost averaging' or something like that—which then proceeded to fall to 10 percent of their original value. I lost my shirt and my nerve. He showed me

all kinds of articles and research to support these purchases and now I read that these people were probably saying these things just to sell stock."

- "We bought an annuity that locked us up for many years and had severe penalties if we chose to change. We were so angry at the person that sold us this annuity that we moved it anyway and took the penalties and set ourselves backward because of it."
- "I have this advisor who is supposed to advise me on my 401(k) but he never calls, and when I call him he offers pretty lame ideas."
- "I had an advisor who told me he was going to put together a 'highly personalized' portfolio to meet my financial objectives. I ran into a couple of other people who had this same advisor and discovered that we all had the exact same 'highly personalized' portfolio. He was essentially doing the same thing for everyone but selling it like a tailor-made process."

These clients' stories reveal associations between investing and gambling, which would certainly act as a caveat regarding the type of language to use when describing your own processes. It is important to note when connecting with other people's stories that the *association* carries more weight than *logic* regarding their behavior. They, in your opinion, may not be responding logically to the experience they describe, but all their future decisions are going to be affected by that event until another event supercedes it in their memory bank.

The association is permanently attached to the experience they describe, and when you bring up a correlating topic, this will be the first story to surface because the brain is now hard-wired to send a synapse in this direction. Mention the word *stock* to the gentleman quoted above who suffered great losses in the market, and you will always stir this association in his mind. This is why it is so important for you as a financial professional to have a broad understanding of the associations your clients or prospects carry regarding the products and services you offer *before* you try to persuade any sort of action. If you forge ahead without understanding these previous experiences, you run the risk of being associated in their emotional story bank with being just like that other person who caused all the problems.

We wouldn't recommend going too far down the path with any prospect without asking about experiences with other providers. Land mines exist and you'll want to complete the sweep before you bring your ideas to the table.

Additional Questions for Investigating Your Client's Financial Experience

- From an A+ to an F, how would you grade your investments so far?
- If you could push the 'reset button' on any financial decision, which one would you choose?
- What's the best investment decision you have ever made? Whose decision was it?
- Which of your friends or relatives have been most successful at investing? Why?

THEIR EXPECTATIONS GOING FORWARD

What are your expectations of me as an advisor?

We first heard this question from veteran financial planner and author John Sestina who would ask it at the end of the first interview with a prospect. John's experience had taught him that it is easier to appoint than to disappoint. We agree that the disappointments would be much sparser if the advisor appointment was clarified.

What exactly do your clients expect from you? What exactly do you expect from your clients? (Some advisors do tell their clients that this is a two-way street and clearly lay out their expectations as well.)

John told us that when clients would begin to describe unreasonable returns on investments or some other criteria of engagement that he could not or would rather not be held to, he would stop the conversation and advise the clients that they might be better off looking elsewhere for the help they desired. This way he was not beholden to client relationships that were destined to disappoint. Another question you may want to ponder with existing clients is What expectations have you created that may be difficult to live up to?

THE TYRANNY OF RETURNS—MANAGING EXPECTATIONS BEYOND YOUR CONTROL

Mark called Mitch for some ideas on how to generate a more positive and enjoyable conversation for his annual meetings with clients. Mitch asked him what he felt was wrong with his current conversations. He answered, "I am so weary of this return on investment discussion. 'How much did I make? How does it compare to this and that index?' It's like the movie *Groundhog Day* where the same thing keeps happening over and over again."

Mitch asked Mark, "How do you suppose *that* conversation got started, and how do you suppose this *context* was created for your relationships?"

"Ouch," Mark replied. "I guess you got me there. It turns out that I pretty much set this expectation in motion, and now it's driving me nuts!"

Suppose you made the following business proposition to your clients: From this day forward I will act as your "weather advisor." Bring me your calendar for next year and choose the days you want to have your outings, picnics, etc., and I'll tell you whether it's going to be sunny or rainy. Are you thinking that we're both running a couple of quarts low with this proposition? If you are, I'd like to ask you what the difference is between this proposition and that of the advisor who promises to beat indexes or returns over which he or she has no control?

This sounds like a formula for stress to us. Advisors who follow this formula are creating an expectation over which they have no control, and then sitting down annually with the client to demonstrate how they have failed.

If your value proposition to clients is to beat the indexes, be sure that you are fully aware that, historically, the odds are against you. With such a proposition you are setting up a risky expectation for your relationships, and that this an expectation that you are answering to on a yearly, if not quarterly, basis. What if instead your semiannual or annual review was not an event to be regarded but rather anticipated as a productive review of jointly held goals, aspirations, and agreements?

Perhaps both the clients and the professional serving them would be better served by using the PROFIT statement approach advocated by the Financial Life Planning Institute. PROFIT stands for *Progress Report On Financial Intentions To date* (see Figure 8.1), which deals only with the issues within the control of the advisor and the client.

With this approach, you can center your review process on the core issues that really matter—your client's concerns and goals—and deal with the numbers that support these core concerns and goals in a peripheral manner. Next to each item you have the opportunity to demonstrate the actions you have taken to help the client make progress in that particular arena of life. The Financial Life Planning Institute's Web-based tool, FLPonline, can customize reports for each of the life concerns and goals of your clients. With this approach, no matter how the markets perform, you will be able to demonstrate progress, which is why the client is coming to you.

FIGURE 8.1 *Sample PROFIT Statement*

P.R.O.F.I.T Statement

Progress Report On Financial Intentions To date

JOE CLIENT

BEGIN

CONCERNS ━━━━━━━━━━━━━ **PROGRESS** ━━━━━━━━

Concerned about an aging parent	• Created a $400 per month income stream • Purchased long-term insurance for your mother, Jackie • Researched assisted living facilities
Develop or review an estate plan	• Started a gifting program for children • Established a charitable remainder trust • Held a family meeting with attorney • Purchased additional life insurance • Purchased key-man insurance for business

GOALS ━━━━━━━━━━━━━ **PROGRESS** ━━━━━━━━

Fund education expenses for a family member	• Researched college choices and assessed costs for daughter, Jill • Set up and began funding a 529 plan for daughter, Jill • Increased funding to son, Jimmy's 529 plan
Get involved in a charitable organization	• Researched charitable organization that serve children's needs in your area • Established an amount of money and time you were comfortable contributing • Initiated charitable gifting and volunteer service for specified charities

© 2004 Mitch Anthony

Question: How often would you like to receive communication and how much communication would you like to receive from me as your personal financial advisor? As you have learned in your practice, not all creatures are equal in the level of communication required to be content with the advisor-client relationship. Some clients need their hands held on a monthly or quarterly basis, others are perfectly satisfied with an annual review, while still others want to hear from you when events require some sort of decision.

We have met advisors who would rather not play soothsayer or assume that their preferred mode of communication is going to satisfy every client. Instead, they ask this question and let the clients outline their preferences. The advisors' job now is to make sure they can meet these expectations. This question simply takes much of the guesswork out of whether clients are happy with the relationship.

QUESTIONS ABOUT YOUR PRACTICE

Much has been written in recent times about the "client experience." This focus on the overall experience of the client can be traced to the seminal work of Pine and Gilmore, whose book, *The Experience Economy* (Harvard Press, 1999), illuminated the evolution of the client expectation in its present form. Pine and Gilmore documented how firms going beyond products and services to providing experiences for their customers are thriving in the present economy.

Firms around the world are paying attention. Are you? What kind of experience, from A to Z, are you providing for your clients? A "blow them away" experience doesn't happen whimsically or by accident. It occurs exclusively by design. Ross Levin, a successful financial planner of Accredited Investors in Minneapolis, Minnesota, uses his Wealth Management Index™ to monitor the client's experience on a yearly basis. Those interested can check out Ross's book by the same name, *The Wealth Management Index*. If you prefer to start today to find out the sort of experience you as a financial advisor are currently providing, you can simply ask, "How am I doing?"

If you don't ask—and pay close attention to the answers— keep in mind that the time is short before someone else in the profession asks your clients how they feel they are being treated, and offers to provide a superior experience.

THE REPORT CARD

We have met some advisors who, in an effort to measure the quality of the experience they are providing, ask their clients to complete an annual report card on how well they are being served. Figure 8.2 is an example of an advisory report card.

Remember that satisfaction does not hinge solely on performance. It must also take into account the level of importance the client places on the particular activity you offer. A Harvard study from 1989 on customer service and delighting clients spoke of the disconnect between satisfaction ratings and how important the issue being rated was to the respondent. It offered a new algorithm for measuring client satisfaction:

$$S \text{ (Satisfaction)} = P \text{ (Performance)} - LOI \text{ (Level of Importance)}$$

Asking clients how satisfied they are with your statements may only give you half the picture. The relative importance of the statements to them must be accounted for to ascertain an accurate satisfaction rating. Using this method, the rating you want in each area is 0. For example, if you receive a 5 for providing clear, easy-to-understand statements and the level of importance of these

FIGURE 8.2 *Advisory Report Card*

Directions: Please rate my performance on your behalf (1 being the lowest, and 5 being the highest).					
Description of Service		**Rating**			
Clear and Understandable Reports	1	2	3	4	5
Importance of Clear and Understandable Reports	1	2	3	4	5
Timely Service and Response	1	2	3	4	5
Importance of Timely Service and Response	1	2	3	4	5
Investment Management	1	2	3	4	5
Importance of Investment Management	1	2	3	4	5
Explaining Risks and Rewards	1	2	3	4	5
Importance of Explaining Risks and Rewards	1	2	3	4	5
Keeping Up to Date with Your Concerns/Goals	1	2	3	4	5
Importance of Keeping Up to Date with Your Concerns/Goals	1	2	3	4	5
Frequency of Contact	1	2	3	4	5
Importance of Frequency of Contact	1	2	3	4	5

© 2004 Mitch Anthony

statements to the client is a 5, then your satisfaction rating in this category would be 0.

If a client rates your statements a 5, but feels that this aspect of the relationship carries an importance rating of 1, the resulting rating of 4 would indicate an overallocation of resources. Translation: You are spending too much for something clients don't really care about.

Again, with this formula a perfect rating in any area is a 0. If your customer service rating is a 5 and the client rates its importance a 5, then your service is right on target.

Instead of just asking, "How am I doing?" you need to ask, "How am I doing on the things that are important to *you*?" If you don't, you can get a great rating from a client who may leave you two months later because you never bothered to find out what issues were most important to him or her.

As noble as it would be to be rated as stellar by all your clients, the most important consideration here is that *you are asking*. You are demonstrating curiosity and the desire to serve and grow your efforts to meet their needs. If you want to really make an impression in a crowded marketplace, make yourself accountable. You'll find that you have very few competitors. Many professionals say they want to provide world-class service, but few offer a platform for perpetual feedback. Our guess is that fanatical curiosity applied to the quality of your performance will be met with admiration, meaningful dialogue, and increased levels of trust.

9

WHERE YOUR CLIENT IS
Mastering the Transitions Inquiry

"There are two sorts of curiosity—the momentary and the permanent. The momentary is concerned with the odd appearance on the surface of things. The permanent is attracted by the amazing and consecutive life that flows on beneath the surface of things."

Robert Lynd, *Solomon in All His Glory*

If you stop to think about it, the products and services you offer have no life—no relevance outside of the transitions that take place in your clients' lives. Life transitions and changes form the vital context that gives breath and life to your ideas and suggestions. Birth, death, college, and retirement are but four of the scores of transitions that play out in your clients' lives at any given moment.

Curiosity's Core Questions

1. What is going on in your life *right now* that could impact your financial situation?
2. Are there others whose lives and lifestyles are impacted by your financial decisions?
3. What grade would you give your financial situation? Why?

Question 1: What is going on in your life right now that could impact your financial situation? Your business can flourish by serving the financial needs attached to the real-time dramas and events playing out in your clients' lives. How much do you know about the current transitions and events in your clients' family, career, finances, and other aspects of their lives? Do you have a disciplined and repeatable process for finding out?

Our discovery processes need to move beyond hit and miss in this area to a point where we have a regular "financial life" checkup on the goings-on and events in clients' lives. For every change in your clients' lives there are necessary financial adjustments and alterations to explore. The financial services industry exists because of the transitions and events in people's lives. Conversations that treat money as a separate, peripheral issue miss both the point and the opportunity. When the conversation commences from the most central and meaningful context in the client's life (what's going on now and the threats and opportunities on the near horizon), your business takes on a whole new meaning in the life of your client.

Ironically, the majority of qualitative discovery questions we found in this industry were not focused first on life in the here and now but on the fuzzy speculations of years to come.

- Where do you want to be in five years?
- What are your financial goals?
- When do you want to retire?

These types of goal-oriented questions asked too early in the conversation do nothing more than form a vaporous, wishful context for our client relationships. They are not rooted in the here and now. There is a time and place for goals questions but it is our conjecture that the time and place for future exploration is *after* you have properly surveyed current realities.

Question 2: Are there others whose lives and lifestyles are impacted by your financial decisions? A derivative of this question— How are others' lives and lifestyles being affected by your financial decisions?—was posed to Kevin by his financial professional. The advisor sensed that Kevin was frustrated with the exchange of time for money he was making in light of the fact that they had two small children at home and that his wife had to travel for her job.

They rolled up their sleeves and analyzed the situation. Kevin was grossing $65,000 per year working in health care. His wife sold software institutionally and made a six-figure income. After taxes and paying for full-time childcare and related expenses, Kevin learned he was netting about $8,500 a year for his toil. Kevin was shocked—but there it was on paper.

His advisor asked, "Is it worth it to you?"

Kevin said, "Absolutely not when I consider the opportunity to spend time with my kids while they are young and to be an active present father in their lives." He also discussed the stress his wife felt leaving on four-day road trips and hoping everything was going fine at the daycare. After discussing this discovery with his wife, they made the decision for Kevin to become a stay-at-home dad for the next three years, after which, he would work part time and be able to see them off to school and greet them when they returned.

Two good questions about the here and now—Who is impacted (and how) by your financial decisions? and Is it worth it to you?—changed the course of this family's lives. We're guessing that they are feeling some deep gratitude toward their advisor for broaching the conversation.

Question 3: What grade would you give your financial situation? Why? No matter what grade clients give you for their current financial situations, it will be important for you to explore further their rationale for the grade. Whether they give their situation an A, C, or F, by asking their rationale for the grade, you'll discover their personal criteria for a healthy financial situation.

You may want to probe further by asking, "Has the influence of any other people affected your grade? If so, who has had an effect on your situation, and how have they affected it?" The answer to this question may be your open door for partnership.

A NUMBERS BUSINESS?

One day after Mitch gave a speech to a financial services audience about the necessity of engaging in a life-centered dialogue with their clients, he was challenged by a veteran advisor who stated with a slightly impudent tone, "You know something, I'm good with the numbers. That is why clients hire me. I get the numbers, I crunch the numbers, and I bring them back in a way that makes sense. I don't need to know all this stuff about their lives."

Mitch was disturbed by this response, not because of the objection itself, but because there seemed to be something missing in this man's rationale that he had failed to address in his speech. This man, by doing a stellar enough job on the left side of the brain, had developed a certain smugness that convinced him that he need not venture into the right side of the client's thoughts (i.e., big picture context, comfort level, etc.).

Mitch sensed that this sort of view of "advisory excellence" existed only because the advisor in question did not fully comprehend either the need for emotional context in his clients' minds or the specific financial implications of their life events and transitions. He believed he could operate in a mathematical vacuum without consequence. Mitch was stirred enough by this challenge to hire researchers to investigate the following question: What events and transitions can possibly take place between the cradle and the grave, and what are the financial implications of those events and transitions?

This research is now entering its fifth year and the results have been nothing less than revelatory. The knowledge harvested in this effort was striking enough that Mitch founded the Financial Life Planning Institute (http://www.flpinc.com) for the purpose of educating the public and the advisor community on the findings. So far, the research has turned up 61 different events or transitions that can or will happen in a client's lifetime. These events and transitions fall into four categories: family events and transitions; career events and transitions; financial events and transitions; and legacy events and transitions.

The paramount finding of the institute's research has been the demonstrable fact that *every single life event and transition has a traceable impact on a client's financial situation.* This leads us to answer the left-brained person's objection that he is doing a great job with the numbers and has no need to advance into inquiry about life with an objection of our own: *If every life event impacts the client's financial state how can you develop a relevant financial plan without understanding the life picture it addresses?*

It simply is not possible to properly address the overall financial situation of any client through statistical processing alone. Avoid the context that these statistics emanate from (their lives), and you lose the larger opportunity to serve. If your only interest is to sell stocks or mutual funds, then you don't need to inquire into the larger context of life. But then again, don't expect your clients to ask you to manage their entire portfolio because you have shown no interest in the context that matters most to them, which is, navigating successfully through life.

For those planners and advisors who wish to be a part of the big picture in their clients' lives, the institute has developed a process that allows advisors to periodically survey their clients' current landscape regarding transitions and events and to present the client with specific financial input that is anchored in each client's particular life transition. Here is an example of how to present the Life Transitions Profile to your clients.

"In my years of experience as an advisor I have noted that, although we do our best to make financial preparations, life does not always comply. Life seems to take its own course with its various twists and turns. I have learned that every time there is a change, that change affects the financial plan. For that reason, I'm now asking all my clients to take a couple of minutes to fill out this Life Transitions Profile (see Figure 9.1). This way we can do our best to make sure that your financial plan is keeping pace with your life."

Once your clients mark the transitions that are going on in their lives, you can prepare customized summary reports for them. Figure 9.2 is a sample of Mitch's summary report.

Here on one page is a list of the important matters in your client's life. Issues of concern from the categories of family, career, financial, and legacy are now pulled to the surface. From here a conversation can ensue that begins like this, "Mitch, out of these transitions you've identified, which one do you feel is the most urgent to work through?"

When Mitch was asked this question, he identified "concern about an aging parent" as the most urgent issue. Mitch and his advisor then looked at the following questions and information around the issue of an aging parent. The report generated a list of general considerations, discovery questions, financial implications, and educational resources based on thorough research for that transition (see Figure 9.3).

Now the client and advisor are having a conversation that uncovers all the needs surrounding this transition or event. The coin drops for the client when you, the advisor, show him the financial implications associated with his life transition. At this point you can say to your client, "Here are the financial issues that need to be considered to successfully manage this sort of concern. I will work to put together some recommendations. In the meantime, you may want to look into some of these educational resources that specifically address this situation."

At this point in the conversation you can point back to the summary sheet of your client's life transitions and say, "The next time we get together which of these other transitions would you

FIGURE 9.1 *Life Transitions Profile*

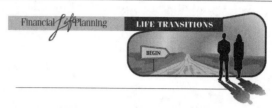

Select the priority level (high, medium, or low) of the life transitions that you are experiencing now or expect to experience in the near future. <u>Leave all others blank.</u>

Personal/Family   Priority Level

Getting married	☐ H ☐ M ☐ L
Going through a divorce or separation	☐ H ☐ M ☐ L
Recent loss of your spouse (widowhood)	☐ H ☐ M ☐ L
Expecting a child	☐ H ☐ M ☐ L
Adopting a child	☐ H ☐ M ☐ L
Need to hire childcare	☐ H ☐ M ☐ L
Child entering adolescence	☐ H ☐ M ☐ L
Child with special needs (disability/other)	☐ H ☐ M ☐ L
Child preparing for college	☐ H ☐ M ☐ L
Child going away to college	☐ H ☐ M ☐ L
Child getting married	☐ H ☐ M ☐ L
Empty nest	☐ H ☐ M ☐ L
Special family event	☐ H ☐ M ☐ L
Providing assistance to a family member	☐ H ☐ M ☐ L
Concerned about an aging parent	☐ H ☐ M ☐ L
Concerned about the health of spouse or child	☐ H ☐ M ☐ L
Concerned about personal health	☐ H ☐ M ☐ L
Family member in need of professional care	☐ H ☐ M ☐ L
Family member with a disability or serious illness	☐ H ☐ M ☐ L
Family member expected to die soon	☐ H ☐ M ☐ L
Recent death of family member	☐ H ☐ M ☐ L
Recent birth of a child	☐ H ☐ M ☐ L
Family member diagnosed with cancer	☐ H ☐ M ☐ L
Entering single parenthood	☐ H ☐ M ☐ L

Work/Career

Contemplating career change	☐ H ☐ M ☐ L
New job	☐ H ☐ M ☐ L
Job promotion	☐ H ☐ M ☐ L

FIGURE 9.1 *Life Transitions Profile, continued*

Work/Career	Priority Level		
Job loss	☐ H	☐ M	☐ L
Job restructuring	☐ H	☐ M	☐ L
New job training/education program	☐ H	☐ M	☐ L
Starting a new business	☐ H	☐ M	☐ L
Gaining or losing a business partner	☐ H	☐ M	☐ L
Selling or closing a business	☐ H	☐ M	☐ L
Transferring business to family member	☐ H	☐ M	☐ L
Downshift/Simplify work life	☐ H	☐ M	☐ L
Taking a sabbatical or leave of absence	☐ H	☐ M	☐ L
Phasing into retirement	☐ H	☐ M	☐ L
Full retirement from current job/career	☐ H	☐ M	☐ L
Buying an existing business	☐ H	☐ M	☐ L
Expanding an existing business	☐ H	☐ M	☐ L

Financial/Investment			
Selling a house	☐ H	☐ M	☐ L
Refinancing your mortgage	☐ H	☐ M	☐ L
Purchasing a home	☐ H	☐ M	☐ L
Relocating	☐ H	☐ M	☐ L
Reconsidering investment philosophy and risk profile	☐ H	☐ M	☐ L
Significant investment gain	☐ H	☐ M	☐ L
Significant investment loss	☐ H	☐ M	☐ L
Concerned about debt	☐ H	☐ M	☐ L
Considering an investment opportunity	☐ H	☐ M	☐ L
Receiving an inheritance or financial windfall	☐ H	☐ M	☐ L
Selling assets	☐ H	☐ M	☐ L
Considering changing financial service provider	☐ H	☐ M	☐ L

Community/Charitable			
Give to other charitable organizations	☐ H	☐ M	☐ L
Monthly stipend to parent(s) (parental pension)	☐ H	☐ M	☐ L
Gifting to children/grandchildren	☐ H	☐ M	☐ L
Develop or review an estate plan	☐ H	☐ M	☐ L
Develop an end of life plan	☐ H	☐ M	☐ L
Creating or funding a foundation	☐ H	☐ M	☐ L
Creating or funding a scholarship fund	☐ H	☐ M	☐ L
Give to community causes/events	☐ H	☐ M	☐ L
Give to church or religious organizations	☐ H	☐ M	☐ L

© 2004, Mitch Anthony

like to discuss?" Voilà, it has just happened—you have adjusted the context of the client relationship going forward. If it was about returns before, those returns just became the peripheral issue serving the larger issue, your client's life situation!

FIGURE 9.2 *Life Goal Summary Report*

Life Transitions Summary Report

Mitch Anthony – February 2005

Transition	Priority
Child Preparing for College	High
Start or Purchase a Business	High
Concern about an Aging Parent	High
Increase Charitable Giving	High
Develop an Estate Plan	High

© 2004 Mitch Anthony

FIGURE 9.3 *Concern about an Aging Parent Report*

Concern about an Aging Parent

Introduction

For the first time in history, large numbers of American families are coping with the care and support of an aging parent. During the last century, increases in the standard of living and advances in medical technology have led to a drastic rise in the number of senior adults. Today, one in eight Americans is over the age of 65 and this number is expected to continue its upward climb in the coming decades. As a result, many families are finding that aging parents are now their top concern.

Most families worry about a parent's finances and living arrangements. Sometimes a retirement pension and Social Security benefits do not cover all the living costs an aging parent faces. In addition, an older person may not be able to keep track of his or her investments and expenses. At the same time there may be questions about an aging parent's ability to care for himself/herself and live independently.

For others, the primary issues are physical and mental health. As we age we become susceptible to more diseases and are often plagued by serious health problems. There are also critical mental disorders that commonly afflict the elderly. We often hear of Alzheimer's, senile dementia, and depression. Each of these requires a specific set of treatments and preventative measures. Many times these become the responsibility of the family.

If you happen to be one of these families there are many resources out there to help. Check out your local library or use the support networks in your community and online. Turn your concerns and anxieties into support and love as you work to provide your parent with valuable care.

General Considerations

- Doctors
- Familiarizing yourself with your parent's needs
- Organizations that can help
- Communicating with your parent
- Communicating with others
- Support for you
- Personnel needs
- Long-term care options
- Legal documents

(continued)

FIGURE 9.3 *Concern about an Aging Parent Report, continued*

Discovery Questions

- How would you describe the current physical and/or mental health of your parent?
- What are your present concerns about your parent's condition? What are your concerns for the future?
- What are your parent's current income sources?
- Do you believe that your parent is living comfortably with the current level of income coming in? Why or why not?
- What type of insurance coverage does your parent have (life, health, long-term care, disability, or others) and where are these policies kept?
- Do you anticipate that your parent will require special care or living arrangements? If yes, have you researched availability and costs associated with the level of care and support needed?
- Do you believe that it will be necessary for you to assist your parent financially? Have you thought through how much you can afford and the best way to go about this? Please explain.
- Are there other family members who could help cover some of the costs involved in providing the necessary care for your parent?
- What changes will you have to make in your personal, family, or work life in order to care for your parent?
- How might these changes affect your long-term goals?

Financial Implications

- Costs related to the needs of your aging parent
- Cash flow planning considerations regarding your aging parent
- Asset management considerations regarding your aging parent
- Debt management considerations regarding your aging parent
- Risk management (insurance) considerations regarding your aging parent
- Tax planning considerations regarding your aging parent
- Estate and legacy planning considerations regarding your aging parent

Educational Resources

1. The Parent Care Solution

Dan Taylor's Web site offers a vast array of useful information regarding The Parent Care Solution: A lifetime program for the health, maintenance, and welfare of parents who may not be able to care for themselves now, or in the future, without destroying the financial or emotional structure of the family.

http://www.parentcaresolution.com/main.html

2. AARP.org: Care and Family

This is a very informative site for anyone interested in providing care for an elderly relative. It includes information on talking about death and dying and how to find the right long-term care facilities for your parent.

http://www.aarp.org/life

FIGURE 9.3 *Concern about an Aging Parent Report, continued*

---

3. U.S. Administration on Aging

The Administration on Aging Web site offers helpful insights on care for aging relatives and suggested support links. Also, you can visit for information on government programs relevant to the elderly, such as prescription drug discount cards and new laws.

http://www.aoa.dhhs.gov

4. Care Guide.com

This is a great source of information on assessing your parent's health care needs and hiring help for your aging family member. Included is a section geared toward the legal and financial issues related to care giving.

http://www.careguide.com

5. Nolo.com

This easy-to-use legal site offers advice on wills, Medicare, health directives, and other legal issues pertaining to elder care. You can also contact experts on the site for answers to your pressing questions.

http://www.nolo.com

© 2005 Mitch Anthony

We continually hear advisors complaining about how they loathe the "tyranny of returns" conversation. The reality we must face is that we created the conversation and established the context for the relationship by telling clients that the goal of "better returns" was the value we could bring. The fact is that much of what happens with returns is out of our control. Conversations about what is happening in our clients' lives, however, are well within our control. This life transitions approach allows us a way to move away from tiresome returns conversations to invigorating and resonating conversations about the things that matter most to the client.

GOING FORWARD

Even if we do our best to prepare financially, life rarely complies. Life takes its own twists and turns. If you choose to use this

Life Transitions Profile, administer it at least once a year to see if anything has changed. One change in life can change everything. Take divorce as an example of that maxim.

Major life events often are times when money is in motion and when many clients switch advisors and begin doing business with someone who knows their stories. Clients slip away when we lose touch with or never make inquiry into what is going on in their world and their lives. You may think you know what is going on in your clients' lives but using a process like this will show you how much you have not yet learned. Needless to say, it's best to be "in the know." When it comes to your client's story it is also best to be in the know in the here and now.

JUST CURIOUS—OTHER QUESTIONS FOR EXPLORING THE HERE AND NOW

- What is the weakest link in your financial picture including debt, income, investments, and plans?
- Is there anything that could reasonably happen that would have the potential to make you wealthy?
- What is the first answer likely to change on your financial questionnaire?
- What has changed in your life since we last met?
- What is the one thing that happened to you during the past few months that made you stop and think, even if only for a few seconds, about your financial security?

10

HOW YOUR CLIENT GOT THERE

Mastering the Principles Inquiry

"When James Burrill Angell, president of the University of Michigan for 38 years, was asked the secret of his success, he answered: 'Grow antennae, not horns.'"

George Sweeting

n the Financial Life Planning Institute's Annual Survey of Client Concerns, we were surprised to learn that reexamining my investment philosophy was in the top five concerns two years running. It was right up there with concern for aging parents and college for children. I guess we shouldn't be surprised—based on events of the last few years—that clients would desire to explore deeper into the issue of the principles and philosophies that guide their money decisions.

Curiosity's Core Questions

1. If I suggested buying 100 shares of Company XYZ, what would be the first three questions you would ask?
2. What are the guiding principles and philosophy that you follow with your money? Who are your main sources of information?

3. Are there any investments you would avoid as a matter of principle?
4. What does your money represent to you? What price or sacrifice was made to earn this money?
5. How do you define true wealth?

If there is any category that we desperately need to "grow antennae" with our clients, it is that deeply personal territory know as principles. *The Oxford Dictionary* defines *principle* as "a fundamental truth or law as the basis of reasoning or action," and, secondarily as, "a personal code of conduct." What are the fundamental truths that guide your client's conduct? Are your client's personal principles a good match for your personal principles? If not, will this individual be a good client?

These are questions financial professionals must consider if they desire to have a sense of "alignment" with their clients. Without clarity in this arena of principles you can end up serving a virtual flea market of mores, whims, values, and expectations that will drive you crazy over time. The principles conversation is intended to help preserve your own sanity as well as set some guideposts for the client's journey.

The questions regarding principles we offer here start with an inquiry into a client's rationale for investment decision making with the question about Company XYZ. The second and third questions about a client's guiding principles and investments he or she might avoid as a matter of principle are aimed at discovering your client's boundaries. It would obviously be in your best interest to know these boundaries *before* you begin making recommendations, lest you find yourself "out of bounds" early on in the relationship. The final two questions go a layer deeper into the realm of emotion, discovering what this money represents to your client, both in terms of the price that was paid to obtain it and what your client hopes that it will provide for her life.

Question 1: If I suggested buying 100 shares of Company XYZ, what would be the first three questions you would ask? The answers you hear will act as an indicator of your client's style of rationale, decision-making models, and criteria for investing. As important as it is to know *what* your clients will invest, you also want to know *why* they would be willing to invest. Possible questions your client would ask include:

- How has the company has been doing lately?
- What does the company do and why do you think its prospects are better going forward?
- Who told you this was a good idea and how often is the individual right about investment tips?
- Who is running the company and how is it ranked as far as great companies to work for?
- How has this company performed for the past few years and has it had the same leadership?
- Is this company producing goods or services that are part of a growing consumer trend?
- What is the stock price?
- Has the company been in any trouble regarding accounting, etc.?

As these questions reflect, your clients possess unique parameters of reasoning that they apply to their investment decisions. Wouldn't it be great it you knew the parameters of reasoning for each of your clients *before* you called them with a product or service, so that you could provide the rationale for the idea? By asking questions about your clients' principles, you can observe your clients' framework of reasoning, make notes in their file for future reference, and check your ideas against their profile of reasoning. This is a simple way to respect how your clients think through and make their investment decisions.

Question 2: What are the guiding principles and philosophy that you follow with your money? Clients may need a moment to think through this question. But their answers will reflect the boundaries they have established based on experience and observation. Consider these examples extracted from client conversations.

- "I would say that never making haste with big money decisions is a guiding principle with my money. My father once told me to be wary of anyone who pressed me to make a quick decision. He said that those who wanted you to hurry rarely had your best interest at heart and, more than likely, had a good reason themselves for wanting you to hurry."
- "I don't believe in investing with borrowed money. I watched a friend lose everything in 2000 with that approach."
- "Live on less than you make, spend only what you need to, and invest in the markets no more than you can afford to lose." (The advisor who got this response is glad he asked this ultraconservative individual about his principles early on in the conversation.)
- "My idea is that you can't get so bound up over investing and saving that you fail to enjoy life today. I believe in setting a percentage that you are going to save and sticking with it. But you can't forget to 'invest' in the here and now as well. You only live once."
- "I don't buy start-ups. I don't buy bio-tech. The bigger the hype the further I run."
- "My philosophy is that I want to know what is most popular right now and then look at strategies for going the opposite direction. My experience has been that not only does the 'herd mentality' rule, but also that the herd usually runs off the cliff together."
- "My philosophy is that I don't want to do anything that could possibly threaten my family's lifestyle if it were to go

wrong. I've got to be able to manage the worst-case scenario without upsetting the quality of life we have built so far."

Every client has idiosyncratic boundaries that are much too abstract to be captured on a risk-tolerance questionnaire. Because these boundaries cannot be measured by a number does not imply that they are fuzzy. In fact, clients are quite clear about many of these philosophical and principle-based boundaries. For many, these are hard and fast rules that are emotionally grounded and best not violated.

Another question you may want to ask in trying to size up your client's guidelines and boundaries for investment decisions is: Who are your main sources of information when it comes to making investment decisions? There are a lot of gurus in the financial decisions landscape and you'll want to know who your client is writing out a check to for financial education—or "financial pornography"—as the case may be. If your client is a big fan of Joe Infomercial with the big hair and his promise of how to get filthy rich without any risk, fees, commissions, or paperwork, you'll probably want to be aware of that fact.

Recently an advisor in the South told me of a prospective client who came to see him and asked, "Do you follow the guidelines of so-and-so because he says such and such?" The advisor answered that although he wasn't "certified" by so-and-so, he followed sound financial principles with all his financial advice to his clients. "The irony," the advisor told me, "was that her portfolio was a mess from following this guru's advice. And that particular fact had not yet settled upon her."

Question 3: Are there any investments you would avoid as a matter of principle? For a couple of years we conducted an informal poll with our advisor and consumer audiences regarding this question. We asked our consumer audiences, "How many of you would like to be asked this question?" About 90 percent of them would raise their hand in the affirmative. When we asked our advisor audiences, "How many of you are asking this question?" we would get indications of less than 10 percent.

While many clients will nonchalantly dismiss any potential of conflict, others will speak with conviction and even resentment about arenas in which they *do not* want their money invested. We have heard stories from the predictable to the bizarre.

- The client who wanted to avoid HMOs because of a traumatic and life-threatening experience
- Those who wanted to avoid tobacco, alcohol, gambling, and other "sinful" stocks
- Those who wanted to screen for environmentally friendly companies and avoid gun manufacturers, etc.
- Those who wanted to avoid companies shipping work overseas
- The client who lost an eye due to an exploding cola bottle and wasn't interested in reinvesting in the company
- The client who had a complaint against a particular manufacturer over a faulty product or an extremely negative experience

This list of criteria could be as long as the list of each client's deeply held convictions. Many clients today buy into the idea of *alignment,* where there is no disconnect between what they believe and feel and how they invest and spend. If you care to inquire further along these lines, there are a number of excellent screening products on the market. There are products that allow the client to lay out definitive criteria which the software then uses to find matches in both equities and mutual fund records along these lines.

Question 4: What does your money represent to you? What price or sacrifice was made to earn this money? In 2000, Mitch's mother called to tell him that she had lost a sizeable portion of her inheritance from her father, a lifetime farmer in North Dakota. She gave Mitch the details of getting tied up in an unadvisable annuity, buying stocks off of Internet tips, and other naïve self-directed investment moves. When she was done with her description of her missteps, he asked her, "All total, how much have you lost, Mom?"

Her answer sent a chill through him. With her voice breaking she said, "I have lost five years of Daddy's work! I just wonder if it was 1947 when we had the tornadoes or 1953 when we had the flood."

She had done the math and calculated the loss not in terms of money but in terms of life expended to create that wealth.

As Mitch often says in his speeches, "That answer sent light from heaven through my soul on the real nature of money in our lives and told me how we can best judge ourselves as financial advisors. We'll know we are great advisors when we measure our clients' money exactly as they do." This is why the fanatically curious stand a much greater chance of becoming great advisors.

Marlin, an advisor in Minnesota, started asking this question of every prospect. One day a man came to his office with a check of almost a half-million dollars and Marlin asked, "What does this money represent to you?"

The man gave him a dead-serious look and muttered, "Four months in traction—and don't you lose one single cent of it!"

That is the kind of information you might want to know *before* you suggest investment vehicles. This question is a good way of getting that critical piece of emotional context.

Question 5: How do you define true wealth? Our favorite definition and answer to this question is: Wealth defined is wealth refined.

SAMPLE OPEN TO A "TRUE WEALTH" CONVERSATION

One suggested opening or setup for this conversation is to set the context with something like this: "In all my years in this business I have learned that it takes more than an account balance or a checkbook to measure wealth. If that were not true there would be no such thing as a happy poor man or a miserable rich man. That is why I like to take the time to ask each of my clients how it is that they define wealth in their life."

At this point you could introduce a questionnaire designed to educe an individual expression of wealth using The Financial Life Planning Institute's True Wealth Questionnaire™ (see Figure 10.1).

This type of conversation allows clients to define wealth in a holistic fashion, which has proven to be a life-changing conversa-

FIGURE 10.1 *True Wealth Questionnaire*

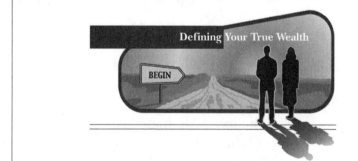

1. How I define success in my working life:

2. How I define success in my family life:

3. How I define balance in my life:

4. How I define success in my financial life:

5. How I hope to be remembered some day:

© 2004 Mitch Anthony

tion for many. Clients have found that the conversation helped to bring clarity to the role of money in achieving the various aspects of wealth that they desire. This conversation opens the door to describing wealth within their family, within their career, and the other aspects of their life, including financial.

Once a client provides this description, the advisor can respond by saying, "This definition of the payoff in your life gives us the guidance we need so that we can use your assets in the best possible manner to bring about this definition of wealth in your life."

We must never lose sight of the fact that behind each story of the accumulation and dispersal of wealth are experiences and events that have shaped our clients' lives and their thinking about money. Those experiences and events have forged certain ideals and principles into place that are now permanently associated with the money. The wise advisor understands this relationship, and the fanatically curious advisor will unearth those ideals and principles before forging ahead.

C h a p t e r

11

WHERE YOUR CLIENT WANTS TO BE

Mastering the Goals Inquiry

"No man ever listened himself out of a job."

Calvin Coolidge

"No matter how smart we are, how well trained we are, it does not give us the right to think for others or, more importantly, to assume how others might feel. We should assume nothing."

Roy Diliberto, CFP

We believe it was Warren Buffett who stated that the only two things that really make you happy are having people who love you and having your health, and money won't buy either one. Of course we always like to balance Warren's maxim with the quote, "Money won't buy you happiness, but neither will poverty." Here is another one of our favorites, "Money doesn't buy happiness. Why, the guy with $10 million is no happier than the guy with nine!"

There is no doubt that it takes more than money to make one happy, but money certainly buys access to a desirable lifestyle and pays for treasured experiences. What those treasured experiences are and what that desired lifestyle looks like is different for every client. It takes conversational skill to draw out a compelling portrait of the client's mind that will be sufficient for future financial discipline. The clearer the image, the more the emotional restraint

116

and discipline that are likely to be applied to the financial plans prepared around that image.

Oftentimes, financial services conversations around the topic of goals stop short of allowing clients to paint a portrait of the life and experiences they desire and instead require clients to pick their choice out of a stack of generic stock pictures (retirement, kid's college education, etc.), or worse, to "paint by numbers" by asking "tired" and overused questions such as, "How much do you think you'll need to retire?" How insipid and unimaginative can a question get?

LIGHTS, CAMERA, CALCULATOR!

Think of the goals conversation like you would about making a movie. If someone came to you and said, "My goal is to make a movie," would your only questions be: "When do you want to make it?" and "How much do you think it will cost?" Would you be curious about what the story was about and how the story was going to end? Would you want to know the names of the actors, the locations, and the various scenes that would be shot? If you were the financier, the producer, or director, you would be required to know *all* of the above.

Think of yourself as the financial planner for the movie, *My Story,* starring your client, and see if that metaphor influences your goals-discovery process. Now we need to know:

- The ending of the movie (What is your ultimate goal in life?)
- The conflicts and how they will be resolved (What issues stand between you and the realization of your goals?)
- The other actors (Which people are important to you, and what are your goals for them?)
- The locations of these scenes (Where do you want to go and where do you want to spend your time?)

Everyone is scripting a feel-good story. Most people are not writing a tragedy, suspense, slasher, or horror film for their lives. They want adventure, romance, and comedy. They want happy endings—and the fact is, the odds are substantially against that happy ending without proper financial preparation. Your clients will need your help for this story to end the way it is scripted. The following is a conversation starter that we think can help you begin to get the "script" you need from your clients. Starters should be worded in such a way as to evoke responses from both the left side of the brain (numbers and logic center) and the right side of the brain (visual and emotion center). Here is a sample opener.

"We all know that there is a vast difference between 'having made it' and 'having it made.' One scenario has to do with a number, and the other with a picture. I'm curious about *your definition* of both the number and the picture. Do you have a number in mind that you would like to reach? If so, how did you come up with that number? Second, do you have a picture in mind of the life you'll be living when you 'have it made'?"

Sit back, listen, absorb, and explore the story of numbers and the number of stories they tell. Try to understand both the story behind the numbers and the numbers necessary to bring their story to life. You'll find this to be an interesting and invigorating dialogue.

GOALS, "SCHMOALS"

Mitch had an unusual experience that reveals a few of the many shortcomings in the way we approach goal-setting and why it often ends up being a nebulous exploration or an exercise in futility.

Mitch went to a workshop where he was encouraged to write down as many goals as he could think of under the heading of "What I want to accomplish within five years." Mitch's goals filled one full side of a page from a legal pad. The instructor exhorted the class on the importance of writing down goals and revisiting them often (maybe even keeping them posted where you would see them every day) as the keys to fulfillment. Mitch took his list home and promptly lost it. Then he completely forgot about the list. He found the list six years later and shares the following comments about his rediscovery:

I'm looking at this list that I prepared with such earnestness six years previous and am rather stunned as two counter-intuitive conclusions about goals jump off of that page. First of all, contrary to the instructor's strict admonitions about keeping that list in front of you, I had already accomplished half of the goals without giving so much as a single glance to this wish list. Second, the other half of the goals I had written down made me wonder what I could possibly have been smoking at the time to think that I actually *wanted* those things!

The lesson I learned from this experience was when we approach goals from a mechanistic, organizational structure (make a list, write down steps, set time lines, etc.), the goals are more organic than they are organizational in their nature. How else could I explain the fact that all these goals had blossomed without me ever cognitively attending them? They were like seeds of direction sown into the garden of subconscious and they simply grew. The ideas that I once thought were goals— but now realize were naïve illusions—did not take root and withered away. Suddenly it dawned on me why I always felt ill-at-ease with the way people went about trying to make goals happen and placing constant pressure upon themselves to make things happen: the whole process always left me with an air of failure. True goals—the things we really want to happen—will take root in our being and will grow and develop at a natural pace. We can do our part by watering and fertilizing the seeds, but we can't push them to become flowers. They have their own necessary pace and rhythm of sprouting and growing.

This experience led to the development of a more organic conversation around goal setting for advisor-client discussions called The Garden of Goals. In this conversation, advisors encourage clients to describe their "seeds" (the things they want or want to accomplish, or experiences and developments they desire) within the specific spheres of family, career, health, leisure, personal growth, legacy, and personal finance (see Figure 11.1). The conversation then asks clients to list the "weeds" (the changes they want to make and situations they need to change) they hope to remove from all these realms as well (see Figure 11.2). The discussion acknowledges the fact that goals (seeds) are more apt to flourish when hindrances (weeds) are removed. If nothing else, this approach gives a new spin on an old topic.

For those who prefer the checklist approach to goals, Mitch and the staff at the Financial Life Planning Institute created the Life Goals Profile, which organizes common goals in the categories of personal/self, family, work/career, leisure/recreation, community/charitable, and legacy that clients can then check off in order to receive personalized advice for their selected goals. See Figure 11.3 for a sample profile.

Through the institute, advisors can then prepare a personalized Life Goals Report (see Figure 11.4) that contains the following: summary, discovery questions about the goal, where to learn more, and a financial life commitment that aids the client in specifying the type of financial commitment they want to make toward accomplishing their stated goals. To quote famed advisor, Deena Katz: "If they are not willing to make a financial commitment toward the goal then it isn't really a goal, it's a whim. If they won't address it financially there is no point in discussing it further."

FIGURE 11.1 *Garden of Goals—Seeds*

GARDEN OF GOALS   **SEEDS**

Stuff I want to have. • Things I want to accomplish. • Who I want to be.

FAMILY

WORK

HEALTH

PERSONAL
(Leisure / Growth / Education)

COMMUNITY
(Charity / Legacy)

PERSONAL FINANCE

FINANCIAL ADJUSTMENTS

© 2004 Mitch Anthony

FIGURE 11.2 *Garden of Goals—Weeds*

GARDEN OF GOALS   **WEEDS**

Changes I want to make. Situations I need to change.

FAMILY

_____
_____
_____
_____

WORK

_____
_____
_____
_____

HEALTH

_____
_____
_____
_____

PERSONAL
(Leisure / Growth / Education)

_____
_____
_____
_____

COMMUNITY
(Charity / Legacy)

_____
_____
_____
_____

PERSONAL FINANCE

_____
_____
_____
_____

FINANCIAL ADJUSTMENTS

_____
_____
_____
_____
_____
_____

FIGURE 11.3 *Goals Profile—Fund a Child's Wedding*

General Considerations

- Location
- Flowers
- Clothing
- Reception
- Transportation
- Other children
- Other sources of funds
- Budgeting

Discovery Questions

- Describe this wedding in as much detail as you can at this time and why you feel it is important to fund it.
- What excites you most about this wedding? Why do you want to be involved in its funding?
- What has been your past experience with weddings and their financial aspects? In particular, have you had any children marry before?
- How much time and money do you plan on committing to fund this wedding?
- In what ways will your funding affect other people around you?
- What sacrifices will you have to make in order to fund this wedding?
- Are there any challenges you will have to face?
- Describe the steps you will take to begin planning and funding the wedding.
- How will such assistance change your life?
- How certain are you that you want to fund your child's wedding?

Financial Implications

- Costs and affordability
- Cash flow
- Assets
- Debt
- Risk management (Insurance)
- Taxes
- Estate/legacy

Educational Resources

1. Bridal Bargains: Secrets to Throwing a Fantastic Wedding on a Realistic Budget, by Denise Fields, Alan Fields

Faced with the fact that the average U.S. wedding costs over $16,000, couples are in need of creative solutions to planning a dream ceremony without a nightmare

FIGURE 11.3   *Goals Profile—Fund a Child's Wedding, continued*

---

price tag. This easy-to-use, entertaining guide comes to the rescue with a wealth of wonderful ideas for that big event. **Barnes & Noble Online**

2. *The Everything Wedding Organizer: Checklists, Calendars, and Worksheets for Planning the Perfect Wedding,* by Laura Morin

Complete with dozens of worksheets, checklists, pockets, and loads of helpful hints, this handy planner features everything a frazzled bride—or groom—needs to get organized. Beginning with setting a date and creating a budget, every aspect of the wedding is covered, right up to the final details. **Barnes & Noble Online**

3. The Wedding Channel

This Web site has a helpful budget center and tools to calculate the costs of any wedding.

http://www.weddingchannel.com

4. The Knot

This wedding planning Web site offers a variety of links to retailers who can supply your needs for the big day. In addition, there are a number of tips, calculators, and checklists to help you and your family prepare.

http://www.theknot.com

© 2004 Mitch Anthony

FIGURE 11.4   *Sample Goals Report*

Life Transition Summary Report
Joe Client, 2/7/2005

Transition	Priority Code
Personal/Family	
Child preparing for college	High
Concern about an aging parent	High
Work/Career	
Starting a new business	High
Financial/Investment	
Reconsidering investment philosophy	High
Community/Charitable	
Giving to other charitable organizations	High
Monthly stipend to parent(s)	High

© 2004 Mitch Anthony

GOAL MINING

There are plenty of available methods for executing an effective goals dialogue. The important issue is to uncover the foundational goals (what a client wants from life) and not just the material objectives (house, car, boat) and other obvious objectives (college, retirement).

Great goals dialogues drill below the surface of superfluity and search for the issues that truly motivate the client. As an advisor, the depth of your goals dialogue will play a significant role in defining the depth and context of your relationship with your client. If you ask only about things and passages, you'll be tied in their synapses to "stuff" and two major events (college and retirement). But, if you drill down into the "stuff" of life—their vision of "having it made"—then, you'll be categorized in their emotional bank as someone who is a partner on that journey as well as being associated with the passages of life and the desired "stuff." Broaden the context of your place in the client's life by virtue of a more comprehensive goals conversation. Following are a few excellent examples we have picked up from successful advisors in our speaking and training tours.

Hakuna Mutata

If you had all the money you would ever need right now, what would you do differently? This is a discussion that can help a client get serious about separating goals from fanciful thought. Like the lottery winners who continue working, many will come to the realization that there are many desirable aspects to the life they have created and comforts they would rather not confuse. This question also helps clients realize that maybe they do not need to wait until they are retired at age 62 or 65 to begin pursuing a design on life that they could live with permanently. While some clients will spin descriptions of elaborate change in response to this question, others will express a sense of gratitude over the many welcome aspects of the life and opportunities they are currently experiencing.

The Million-Dollar Bill

One advisor has a million-dollar bill on his desk that he hands to the client or prospect as a conversation starter. He asks the following:

1. If you won $1 million in the lottery, what would you do with it?
2. What wouldn't you do with it?
3. If you had a chance to donate it to charity, which would you give it to?
4. What would you have done with the money if you had won it the year you graduated?

This million-dollar dialogue can prove interesting and informative to both advisor and client as it provides the following:

- The client's immediate goals (What would you do with it?)
- The client's observations regarding money mistakes (What wouldn't you do with it?)
- The client's heartfelt concerns (Whom would you give it to?)
- How far the client has come (What would you have done with it back then?)

Fast Forward

We are 30 years off into the future. Looking back, what do you hope to have accomplished for yourself and for others? An interesting perspective to bring to the goals dialogue is that of looking *backward* instead of looking *forward*. It has been well said that no man ever lay upon his deathbed and lamented that he had not spent more time at the office. Retrospect carries within it a powerful ability for clarification and refinement, separating "true gold" goals from those made of fool's gold.

You could also administer this conversation on paper to give the client the opportunity to think through their goals for themselves and for others (see Figure 11.5).

Enough Is Enough

How much is enough? Isn't this the ultimate question to ponder regarding the wealth-building process? It is likely that no two answers will be the same. It is unlikely that the answer will come in numerical form. Most of the time when you ask this question, you will hear answers that touch on aspects of Abraham Maslow's

FIGURE 11.5 *Mission Accomplished*

MISSION ACCOMPLISHED

Place yourself 30 years down the road and you are looking back on your accomplishments. What goals and objectives do you hope to have accomplished in these three decades?

FOR MYSELF: _____

_____

_____

FOR OTHERS: _____

_____

_____

© 2004 Mitch Anthony

Hierarchy of Needs: security, safety, love, freedom, self-esteem, and self-actualization.

How much is enough ranks in our minds as an important conversation. If no other conversation to this point has taken the dialogue past the numbers to the ultimate end they are designed to achieve, this conversation should do it. Ultimately, we want both the number and the emotional rationale for that number to best be able to serve our clients. The number and the number's *raison d'être* provide a snapshot from both sides of the client's brain and indicate the agenda by which your performance will truly be evaluated in the long run.

If the client tells you that no amount is enough, then you have a decision to make about the price you will end up paying trying to keep that client happy.

For most of us "enough" is about doing the things we want with our lives, taking care of those we love, living without long-term fear and daily anxiety, and having the opportunity to make choices when opportunities are presented. This is "the life" that most people hope for and should be the big-picture focus of an effective goals dialogue.

Other Questions You Can Ask

- If you had to write a one-sentence mission statement with regard to your investing, what would your mission statement say?
- It's 11:00 on Wednesday and you're 70 years old. What are you doing?
- If you had an all-expenses-paid vacation, where would you go?
- Do you have any goals for your children and grandchildren?
- Describe the dream house you will live in when you're 65.
- List three goals you have yet to accomplish in your lifetime.

12

THEY MEAN BUSINESS
Dialogues with the Small Business Owner

"Bill Clinton was one of the most gifted American political figures in modern times. Trust me, I learned this the hard way. . . . He devoured ideas with an insatiable curiosity and then pursued them with unbounded energy and infectious enthusiasm."

Former President George H.W. Bush, on competing with Former President William J. Clinton

The pride in John's eyes was apparent as he described how, over 55 years ago, his grandfather had started a small construction firm in a small Midwestern city. He founded the company on the principles of dependability and pride in workmanship. Dependability meant that employees showed up on time, they finished the job as promised, and the only subcontractors that were hired had as much pride as they did. His grandfather's

A SMALL BUSINESS DEFINED

A small business, as defined by the U.S. Small Business Administration, is one that has no more than 500 employees for most manufacturing and mining industries and no more than $6 million in annual sales for non-manufacturing industries. The nearly 23 million small businesses are a driving force in the U.S. economy, accounting for 40 percent of the nation's private sales and 99.7 percent of all employers. (Grove and Prince) company had taken great pride in constructing buildings to last, and the company had continued this tradition. John often drove around town and marveled at how his family had worked hard to fill their city with schools, factories, hotels, and office buildings. This has always been more than just a business to his family and they see themselves as an integral part of the history and growth of this community.

John's emotional description of the ethical foundation of his business was not the result of a random conversation but a well-designed discovery dialogue used by Dave, a financial advisor whose specialty is assisting businesses in the building trades. The historical perspective and pride of ownership that poured from John was in response to Dave asking, "What principles and values have you and your family focused on in building this business to the place it is today?"

Dave learned early on in his advisory career that each small business he was trying to serve was a part of a larger genre of business; that is, doctors and dentists in health care, motel and restaurant owners in hospitality, builders and subcontractors in construction, shop owners in retail, etc. He wrestled with the question that many advisors struggle with, Is it more advantageous to be a generalist to the masses or a specialist to a specific group?

He quickly became a student of the construction trade, the financial vagaries of building a business, the liabilities involved, the intricacies of finding and keeping good help, and the challenges of selling the business or creating a succession plan. He began there because that's where his best relationships were and because he had friends in the business that were willing to teach him the ins and outs of survival and success in the construction trade.

He soon found that business owners loved talking to people who understood their idiosyncrasies and who fluently could speak their industry jargon. He positioned himself against competitors as someone who had chosen to master a specialty rather than specialize in generalities. He found a willing audience and the idea grew upon itself.

You may wonder why we are opening this chapter on discovery with business owners with a strategic bent. There is a simple explanation. The more you know about the particular business and the larger industry it competes within, the more specific you will be in your discovery dialogue, which will result in impressing prospects from the start with the informed and intelligent nature of your questions. We believe that your level of curiosity will determine your ferocity as a competitor in the lucrative and fast-growing small business advisory business. Just as former president George H.W. Bush admitted that he was bested in competition by Clinton's "insatiable curiosity, unbounded energy, and infectious enthusiasm," you can have your competitors saying the same about you. But it all starts with curiosity. Curiosity fuels the energy and enthusiasm.

The more you ask, the more you know. The more you know, the more strategically intelligent you become. The more strategically developed you become, the greater the distance becomes between you and your competition. This is especially true when attempting to carve out a niche in the business-advisory space. People in business want to work with someone who knows their business and who offers "signature solutions."

According to Chip Roame of Tiburon Strategic Advisors, this is the pattern of some of the most successful advisor practices in America. He cites the examples of Sacramento-based Hanson and McClain that manages billions of dollars for telephone company retirees. About half of the company's 2,000 clients are Pacific Bell retirees and they believe they have captured about 70 percent of the market with their specialized approach. Another example would be the Milwaukee-based firm Cleary Gull that developed a customized program for pilots. They have produced customized seminars for the pilots of leading airlines and use the language of pilots (engineering, safety, staying on course) in introducing their services. Both of these firms engaged in deep discovery of the industry they sought to serve and the issues people in those industries face with their financial future.

DYNAMIC BUSINESS DISCOVERY

First, before you begin inquiry with business owners, we would like to remind you that a business is not a thing as much as it is a living, breathing thing. Treat it like an organism instead of an organization. A business operates more like a human body than it does like an industrial machine. Its circulatory system or lifeblood is its relationship to its customers. Its nervous system is how well it communicates internally. Its digestive system is concerned with its consumption and waste of resources. Its muscular system is its people and ability to attract and retain good people. Its skeletal system is comprised of the properties and possessions that the business relies on. The respiratory system is concerned with its cash flow and debt management and how much breathing room the business has. The immune system provides protection for all the other systems and is concerned with outside threats and liabilities that could hinder or harm the business.

It might help you earn credibility with a business owner to bring this organization versus organism perspective to the table and remind the business owner of the dynamic nature of his or her business and industry and the advantage of having a financial consultant who keeps in touch with those changes and who can respond quickly.

Second, we would like to encourage you to take a good, hard, scrutinizing look at the particular context you create for your advisory services when describing your value proposition to business owners. The questions you ask will, to a large degree, either constrict or expand the role you play in the business owner's plans.

We have met advisors who position themselves as financial coaches, and others who position themselves as chief investment officers or as consultative chief financial officers to businesses too small to have one of their own (but big enough to have multitudinous financial needs).

Keep in mind the Financial Life Planning model of inquiry we offered for discovering the individual lives of your clients because it applies here as well as to the story behind the business. The path for discovery is history, transitions, principles, and goals.

For the purposes of getting to know the business owner, gaining perspective on the world, learning what matters most to the business owner, and understanding the context that this business was created in and continues to compete in, we offer the following inquiries from the Life of Your Business™ inquiry.

History

- How did you get started in this business?
- How did you get from there to here?
- What have been the greatest benefits and the greatest costs of running your own business?

Transitions

- What challenges do you face in running your business today?
- What are the greatest challenges facing your industry?

Principles

- What would you like people to be saying about your business 20 years from today?
- If you could pass on one lesson to people thinking of starting their own business, what would that lesson be?

Goals

- What are your goals for selling or passing this business on some day?
- Are there other mountains you would like to climb?

THE STEVE JOBS FACTOR: "HOW DID YOU GET STARTED?" AND THE HISTORY INQUIRY

The business you see is the animation of somebody's dreams—the incarnation of blood, sweat, and tears, paid for with a price greater than money, upon which hang the hopes of many. Every business has a unique story and every business owner has a story to tell.

This history inquiry seems to be irresistible for business owners. They all have a story to tell and enjoy telling it. Like the legendary Steve Jobs assembling computers in his garage and Michael Dell doing the same in his dorm room, or Nike's founder Phil Knight selling shoes out of the trunk of his car, business owners have dreamed of doing something on their own, taking calculated risks, enduring discouragement and adversity, scratching their way through humble beginnings, and taking tremendous pride in their accomplishments.

The more you know of this story, the better positioned you will be in terms of helping the owner fulfill his dreams for this business. This story is an irreplaceable piece of context that you will need to know if you have any intention of participating in the big picture of this business plan going forward.

Once you have given the business owner the opportunity to share the story of his or her early vision, humble beginnings, and struggles along the way, you may wish to delve further into the makeup of and nature of this individual by asking questions such as:

- Why did you go into business on your own?
- If you could do it over again, would you do it differently?
- What have been the greatest benefits and costs of running your own business?

And to gain greater insight into the makeup and nature of the business, you can ask questions such as:

- What were the greatest challenges and obstacles you faced when starting this business?
- How have you had to adapt and adjust through the years to stay competitive?

The stories you hear are a critical prologue to the business realities you will discover upon further inquiry into the present realities and challenges this business owner faces. Business owners will be much more willing to share these present realities and challenges with you once they sense that you understand the historical context of their business and original vision.

CHALLENGES AHEAD: THE BUSINESS TRANSITIONS INQUIRY

Every business and business owner faces continual challenges. There aren't many "autopilot" businesses out there; subsequently, the business owner is forced to deal with fresh challenges and constant adjustments. Some of these adjustments are financially oriented.

What are the chances of business owners informing you of every change and transition going on in their businesses in ample time for you to be able to bring some valuable service or advice? Business owners are caught up in the everyday functions of running their businesses just like you are with your business.

Position yourself as a financial consultant who helps business owners step back from the fray to strategically analyze how the various systems of their businesses are working. Communicate that, as a business owner, you understand the dynamic nature of business and the pitfalls of being so busy working *in* the business that you often lack time to work *on* the business. Most business owners appreciate the opportunity to step back from the day to day to discuss the big picture with someone who understands the importance of looking ahead and in viewing the separate pieces as parts of the whole.

This need to work *on* the business is pervasive across the small business landscape and pulsates like an open wound for many entrepreneurs who have become victims of their own creations.

THE E-MYTH

Witness the proliferation of the "coaching" industry with regard to business owners who feel as if their businesses are now running them. A specific example of this phenomenon is the ongoing success of Michael Gerber's *The E-Myth* coaching program, which targets business owners struggling with how to balance the manifold responsibilities of running a business.

In his book, *The E-Myth,* Gerber describes the individual who is good at a particular skill—for example, making pastries—and wakes up one day as a owner of a pastry business, spending very little time doing what he or she loves, overwhelmed by managing people, administrating operations, accounting concerns, receivables and collectibles, sales and marketing, etc., and wonders if it was all worth it. *The E-Myth* is Gerber's term describing the illusion that, because you excel at a particular skill, you are cut out to be an entrepreneur.

A QuickBooks survey also revealed that small businesses continue to be challenged by many of the day-to-day activities associated with running a business. One-third of those polled felt that accounting was the most intimidating part of running their businesses—beating out employee management, customer relationships, or inventory and sales. Only 6 percent identified themselves as having "a lot" of formal training, and more than half said they had none. (Source: "Survey Shows Optimism among Small Businesses Despite Economic Concerns," Intuit press release, December 20, 2002.)

Most small business owners need a lot of help but have a hard time trusting others, delegating work, and taking their hands off of any part of their precious investment. If you can walk into a conversation with small business owners and demonstrate the sort of value that will help them to free up both time and stress and help them to keep up on the global financial issues within their business, you will have engaged entrepreneurs.

Do you want to open up a larger context for your conversations with business owners? Ed Howat, director of wholesale training at Nationwide Insurance, understands the dilemma of small business people caught up in activities that are not necessarily helping their business grow. For example, he will schedule a meeting and ask a business owner to bring him eight envelopes, each containing a check for $250. He tells the owner that he's going to make a trade with her that he thinks she's going to like. He also has eight envelopes that he trades with her. When the business owner opens the eight envelopes she received, she finds that for every $250 check she gave to him, he gave her a $20 bill. Of course, she tells him she's been ripped off, to which he tells her that's the way many business owners conduct business every day. They commit $250 worth of value and skill each hour to a job they can hire someone else to do for less than $20 an hour.

Allison Mnookin, a small business expert at Intuit, suggests to small business owners that they should look into working with a financial advisor or accountant to identify new opportunities to improve business processes or identify new revenue streams. She also suggests that business owners take stock of their daily work routine and look for ways to free up more of their time, noting that "the owner's time is often one of the most valuable commodities that a business has." With more time, a business owner or manager can focus on finding new customers or better serving existing ones—both of which can help improve the business's bottom line.

It seems that one of the most productive business conversations comes back to the old maxim that time is money, and nowhere is that truer than with the owner's time. Why not start an investment discussion with the premise that how you invest your time is the link to having more money to invest?

CHALLENGES AND CHANGES

What are the biggest challenges and most taxing changes facing your small business clients today? Are you having conversations with these business owners regarding the products or services you have to offer, or about the road ahead that they want to traverse? Figure 12.1 highlights a study conducted by the National Federation of Independent Business (NFIB) and indicates some of the challenges in our modern business environment.

A BETTER BUSINESS CONVERSATION

Here is a conversation overheard between a financial advisor and a small business owner:

"So, how's business these days?"
"Going well."
"Keeping pretty busy then?"
"Yeah, keeping busy."

FIGURE 12.1 *Problems Cited by Small Business Owners*

Rank	Problem
1	Cost of Health Insurance
2	Cost and Availability of Liability Insurance
3	Workers Compensation Costs
4	Cost of Natural Gas, Propane, Gasoline, Diesel, Fuel Oil
5	Federal Taxes on Business Income
6	Property Taxes
7	Cash Flow
8	State Taxes on Business Income
9	Unreasonable Government Regulations
10	Electricity Costs
58	Interest Rates
64	Credit Rating
68	Obtaining Long-Term Business Loans
70	Obtaining Short-Term Business Loans

Source: *Small Business Problem and Priorities*. National Federation of Independent Business Research Foundation. 2004.

"I wanted to come over some time and show you some investment options for the cash that sits for a long time in money market accounts. Do you want to get together and look it over?"

"Give me a call at my office and I'll look at my schedule, or go ahead and drop something in the mail."

Do you think we can do better than the launching pad of "How's business these days?" That question is the business equivalent of the benign, social greeting, "How are you?" Nobody expects a real answer to that question. If you are in a social setting where there isn't going to be time to have a substantive conversation, you might be better off asking individuals how they are or how a member of their family is, than to inquire about the pulse of their business. Set yourself up for more meaningful conversations by making sure there will be sufficient time once the dialogue turns substantive.

Think about opening your business conversations with something more provocative and compelling—something that is rooted in genuine curiosity. You could enjoy much more lively and compelling dialogue by launching with questions like:

- What changes have you seen in your business in the last year?
- What is happening these days in the _____ (fill in the blank) industry?

For those who want to establish themselves as a financial consultant to businesses it would be helpful to use a method of inquiry that gives a broader, more global picture of what is going on in their business. The following inquiry instrument, The Business Transitions Profile (see Figure 12.2), is a methodology much like the personal life transitions inquiry but geared toward changes and contemplated changes in a business.

You can begin the discussion of The Business Transitions Profile by saying: "The way we like to help business owners is by engaging in 'financial scanning' before we engage in financial planning. To do a good job at financial planning you have to have a good idea of what is going to happen or what you want to happen. This is where financial scanning comes in—taking a yearly x-ray, if you will, of the changes that are going on or are anticipated in your business. This profile will help us to get a portrait of what is happening and enable us to develop recommendations that fit where you are at and where you want to go."

This sort of big-picture inquiry can help you in your efforts to establish a consultative role with business owners. By keeping in touch with the dynamics of their businesses and industries and finding solutions that address where their businesses are at any given period, you are tying yourself and your services to the life of those businesses. Keep in touch with the changes and the contemplation of changes and soon you will find that they will be calling

FIGURE 12.2 *Business Transitions Profile*

Employees

Transition	Priority	Time Frame
☐ Hire a new employee		
☐ Fire an existing employee		
☐ Offer early retirement package		
☐ Outsource to temp agency		
☐ Replace health or dental plan		
☐ Establish health or dental plan		
☐ Replace qualified retirement plan		
☐ Establish qualified retirement plan		

Growth / Contraction

Transition	Priority	Time Frame
☐ Create or change business structure		
☐ Eliminate a product or service		
☐ Sell off product or service		
☐ Offer new product or service		
☐ Purchase a competing business		
☐ Sell an existing business unit		
☐ Form strategic partnership or joint venture		
☐ Refurbish / update facility		

Sales & Marketing

Transition	Priority	Time Frame
☐ Open up a new market		
☐ Close an existing market		
☐ Launch a new ad campaign—create plan and/or hire an agency		
☐ Constrict sales force		
☐ Expand sales force		
☐ Increase or decrease sales incentives		

(continued)

FIGURE 12.2 *Business Transitions Profile, continued*

Financial Transitions

Transition	Priority	Time Frame
☐ Raise capital—business loan		
☐ Raise capital—private offering		
☐ Raise capital—public offering		
☐ Raise capital—private loan to business		
☐ New business investment—expansion		
☐ New business investment—building		
☐ New business investment—equipment		
☐ Offer credit to customers/clients		
☐ Invest free capital		
☐ Create future income stream		

Risk Management

Transition	Priority	Time Frame
☐ Business insurance to protect assets		
☐ Protect business from loss of key employees		
☐ Protect family from business liabilities		
☐ Ensure earnings for owner(s)/key employees		

Advisory

Transition	Priority	Time Frame
☐ Hire/change a bookkeeper or CPA		
☐ Hire/change an attorney to represent business		
☐ Hire/change a financial advisor		
☐ Hire/change a business coach		

Business Succession

Transition	Priority	Time Frame
☐ Create a buy-sell agreement		
☐ Purchase key-man insurance		
☐ Plan to sell business to key employee(s)		
☐ Plan to sell business to outside interest		
☐ Plan to sell business to family member		

© 2005 Mitch Anthony

you *before* they contemplate making changes to discover what the financial implications might be.

IN A PERFECT WORLD

What would the ideal business scenario look like for you in terms of size and personal workload? One business owner told us that he recently sat down and figured out how much his business was netting and realized that he wasn't netting any more than he had been seven years ago when he had a simpler and smaller operation. His business had grown, but so had his expenses and the amount of energy and time he had to put into it.

It's probably not safe to assume that everyone wants to be the Bill Gates of their industries. Some business owners would simply like to build a steady and manageable business without the complications that scale and expansion bring. Instead of assuming that every person is looking to build a large-scale operation, some day open the door to discovery by asking them to describe their ideal business scenarios in terms of size and personal involvement. Every vision for business is as unique as the person(s) starting the business. Take time to explore that vision.

ALL IN THE FAMILY—FROM SUCCESS IN BUSINESS TO BUSINESS SUCCESSION

What are your goals for selling or passing on the business some day? Small business owners have a very different menu of financial needs than do other affluent investors, including business succession plans, key-person insurance, and buy/sell agreements. One thing they do have very much in common with other affluent investors is the fact that many of those plans are incomplete or outdated.

"Our research showed that many of their needs were not addressed: Less than half had buy/sell agreements, and those who did had not updated them in more than eight years; one-third did not have key-person insurance; almost half lacked a succession plan; less than one-fifth had an asset protection plan; and their estate plans hadn't been updated in more than a decade."

Prince and Grove, July 2004, *Financial Advisor* magazine

Russ Alan Prince and Associates conducted a study that examined the financial lives of 603 business owners, their use of products and services, and their relationship with their financial advisors. Of the 603 small business owners in the study, 387 ran family businesses and the other 216 operated corporate small businesses. To qualify as a family business, the firm had to have one or more family members employed in a senior position, one or more generations involved in the business, and majority ownership. The business owners in the study had an average net worth of $11.7 million and average investable assets of $1.5 million. In each case, both groups ranked taking care of heirs at the top of their list, but it was a greater concern for family business owners. As to the differences between concerns of family-owned and corporate-owned businesses, the study concluded that estate taxes were a higher priority for family businesses because the estate included the business and estate taxes are directly linked to succession issues. The study also stated: "Both family and corporate businesses were more or less equally concerned about being sued and making charitable gifts, which speaks to their need for asset protection plans and advanced planning guidance."

So therein lies your opportunity. If you want a long-term, big-picture relationship, the end is always a good place to start a conversation, especially with the business owner. *What is the ultimate payoff you are looking for in building this business?* Be assured that the payoff has something to do with keeping some money and passing other monies on. The more specific this discussion becomes around the end game, the better positioned you will find yourself in the present.

ACT II

Are there any other mountains you would like to climb? Legend has it that when Edmund Hillary, the beekeeper from New Zealand, was asked why he wanted to scale the tallest peak in the world, he answered, "Because it is there." When talking to business owners about retirement, succession, or selling or liquidating their business, keep in mind that it took a healthy ego and an abundance of energy to build that business, and that ego and energy may be looking for a sequel act.

They possibly have shelved some dreams or postponed some pursuits because of the daily demands of running a business. Once they transition out of their businesses, they are free to seek out new opportunities to address those dreams and pursuits. If you want to be a part of their picture going forward, find out what the next scene looks like. This question can help you do that.

13

THE NEW RETIREMENT DIALOGUE

The New Retirementality requires a shift both in how we plan our lives and how we manage our resources. The work we must do is part philosophical and part fiscal. Once we recognize retirement for what it is, an artificial finish line, we can discard the old model and expectation and move on to designing a fulfilling life. Reclining giving way to redefining, retiring giving way to rewiring, a life of nothing but recreation giving way to a life of re-creation, this is the New Retirementality.

From *The New Retirementality* by Mitch Anthony

NEW RETIREMENT REALITIES

What was originally intended to be a one-year bridge from the loading dock to the eternal loading dock (when the retirement age was set at 62 in 1937, life expectancy was 63) has now become a third stage of life lasting up to 30 years or longer. As one 85-year-old told us, "I've now spent as much time in my retirement career as I did in my 'real' career." Well, the retirement career is now becoming as real as the first, with a different sort of design, of course. Fewer hours working. More inclination toward doing what you really enjoy. Working with causes and individuals you enjoy as well.

Eighty-five percent of baby boomers have indicated that they want to "die with their boots on" and be engaged somehow until their dying day. They don't want the old corporate routines, the politics, the overly demanding, life-out-of-balance schedule, but they do want to be engaged, valued, respected, fruitful, and relevant. The time has come for a new conversation to replace the weatherworn, "How old are you and how much do you have?" conversational algorithm that has seen its better days.

We can assure you that this new generation of third-agers—one baby boomer is turning 59½ every seven seconds in 2005 and continuing for the next 20 years—is paying attention to the keys to successful aging research that is proliferating at this moment in history. These individuals are paying attention to the keys for successful aging in their bodies (diet, exercise, and activity), their minds (challenge and curiosity), and their souls (purposeful engagement and giving back). Shouldn't your retirement dialogues pay attention to these factors as well?

Look at their focus and the trends they spell. The focus on curiosity is resulting in more people "retiring" in university towns and going back to school—a renewed focus on self-improvement and self-actualization. The focus on challenge is resulting in new horizons in the 65+ age group—more people are working because they want to, and there is an increased awareness to exercise the brain like any other muscle lest it atrophy. The focus on purposeful engagement is resulting in record numbers of new charities and foundations and a deep need to make a lasting mark in the world. This topic and the dialogue surrounding it will be dealt with at length in Chapter 14, "Bring Meaning to My Money."

Here's are four questions you can ask:

1. What observations have you made and what lessons have you learned from watching others retire?
2. Are you sure you want to fully retire?
3. What will your life in retirement look like?
4. How do you feel you can make the most of the years ahead of you?

Question 1: What observations have you made and what lessons have you learned from watching others retire? By asking this question, you allow your clients to articulate, first and foremost, what they *don't* want their retirement to look like and, subsequently, begin thinking about the successful retirees they have observed. This question has proven to be a great conversation starter and gets stories flowing about the dos and don'ts of successful retirement living. Here are some examples of responses to this question.

- "My grandfather never enjoyed any leisure. He was saving it up for the time he would retire. Six weeks into retirement Grandma had a stroke and they never took a trip in their RV."
- "I lived for years in a railroad town and remember vividly the guys who retired at 60, sat around bored out of their minds, and died by 61 or 62. You could pretty much count on it."
- "My father is a lawyer and still goes to work every day and says he would have died ten years ago without it."
- "When I saw the tension that my parents had in their home upon retirement, I knew that wasn't going to be the way I would do it. I will make sure I'm not sitting around the house getting old and grumpy."

Question 2: Are you sure you want to fully retire? Roy Diliberto, CFP, tells the story of one of his clients who was planning to sell his company to one of the people that worked for him and then retire. Roy noticed, however, that he seemed to be struggling with the whole proposition during the meeting. Everyone at the meeting, including lawyers and accountants, wanted to focus on the numbers and the sale of the business. Roy had the intuitive insight to realize that this conversation needed to transcend to a different plane.

Roy asked this client what he loved and hated about his work. The client glowed when he talked about the aspect of work that he loved. "Buying vehicle parts!" he beamed. He had spent a lifetime of expertise in buying used parts, reconditioning them, and reselling them at a wonderful profit. Nobody knew more about reselling vehicle parts than this man. The negatives were the day-to-day operational details and tasks that had worn away his patience and energy level.

Roy brought a novel perspective to the discussion by asking, "Instead of selling the business to this employee, why don't you give him a $100,000 raise and let him manage the operational side of the business, and you can continue to buy and make deals on a part-time basis?" The client about came out of his chair with excitement. His whole countenance changed—he loved the idea!

The accountant broke in with a question about the agreement of sale (as if the preceding conversation had never happened or that the dialogue was just a fantastical romp in Never Land). The client, flushed red with frustration at the dismissive actions of the accountant, pounded the table, pointed at Roy, and stated sternly, "No! I want to do what *he* said."

The accountant represents the mindset in this industry that cannot think outside of the numbers and the traditional retirement box. But this client was clearly a man who would not be truly happy unless his phone was ringing. The conversation Roy started is what the New Retirementality is all about for the financial advisor. By asking a few questions, advisors are in a position to help clients rethink the retirement proposition and come to a solution that pays both materially and emotionally.

The enjoyment of work and the desire to stay involved to some degree is by far the greatest motivation for the oxymoron "working retiree." Many retirees are bored. Many miss the engagement of challenge, competition, and networking with others. This is a trend that will only continue.

Question 3: What will your life in retirement look like? Far too many retirees are adrift on a sea of aimlessness, boredom, and discontentment. They found their freedom from the old job and the old routines but didn't sufficiently contemplate what that freedom could lead them toward.

There is an entire generation of people arising who have decided to make the "third age" of life the most meaningful. This group understands the habits, attitudes, and pursuits that directly correlate with successful aging and staying young at heart. Words like *curiosity, connectivity, challenge,* and *contribution* are hallmarks of a new generation of retirees, who are transforming retiring into refiring and reclining into refining. These people are leaving an indelible impact on the people, the ideas, and the causes they care most about.

Following are three retirement discovery tools used in Mitch's Retiring on Purpose program. The first, "The Ideal Week in Retirement" (see Figure 13.1), is great for helping clients see that planning how to spend their time in retirement is as big an issue as planning how to spend their assets. In fact, the former must happen first to ensure the latter is viable. The second, "The A/B List" (see Figure 13.2), will help clients identify specific goals that you can start planning for. The third, "The Exploration Agenda" (see Figure 13.3), opens up dialogue about places they would like to go, experiences they have dreamed of having, people they would like to meet, and skills they would like to learn.

These types of conversations help clients ponder the possibilities of the emancipated life ahead. As one advisor tells his clients, "It's a time to move from the 'someday list' to the 'today list.'" He

FIGURE 13.1 *The Ideal Week in Retirement*

Spending Your Time	**The Ideal Week in Retirement**		
	Morning	**Afternoon**	**Evening**
SUNDAY			
MONDAY			
TUESDAY			
WEDNESDAY			
THURSDAY			
FRIDAY			
SATURDAY			

"Your most valuable asset is time, not money. A rich life is about spending that time well." — Mitch Anthony

5

FIGURE 13.2 *The A/B List*

FOR EVERYTHING THERE IS A SEASON

Select five choices from the list below that best describe your next phase of life and place on your (A) list. Place your second five choices on the (B) list.

I SEE RETIREMENT AS A TIME TO:

• Travel	• Continue present work	• Dust off old dreams
• Relax	• Find balance	• Do consulting work
• Teach others	• Play	• Increase my
• Spend time with spouse	• Mentor others	community involvement
• Explore	• Connect with friends	• Hang out with retired friends
• Learn new skills	• Educate myself	• Help others
• Connect with family	• Work with charities	• Connect with a cause
• Engage in a hobby	• Help out with kids	• Get a part-time hobby job
• Do projects at home	• Take it easy	• Take on a new challenge
• Start a new business	• Go back to school	• Write about experiences

(A) LIST

• _____

• _____

• _____

• _____

• _____

(B) LIST

• _____

• _____

• _____

• _____

• _____

"There is a big difference between 'having made it' and 'having it made.'" — Mitch Anthony

FIGURE 13.3 *Exploration Agenda*

EXPLORATION AGENDA

PLACES I WOULD LIKE TO GO:

  1. _____
  2. _____
  3. _____

EXPERIENCES I WOULD LIKE TO TRY:

  1. _____
  2. _____
  3. _____

SKILLS I'D LIKE TO LEARN:

  1. _____
  2. _____
  3. _____

PEOPLE I'D LIKE TO MEET:

  1. _____
  2. _____
  3. _____

"Having exciting agendas on the horizon infuse people with hope and a joy of living." — Mitch Anthony

© 2003 Mitch Anthony

asks his clients, "Do you have any things that you always told yourself, 'someday when I can, when I have time, I'm going to . . . ?' Now is the time in your life to think about doing those things while you have freedom, mobility, and the energy to do them."

Question 4: How do you feel you can make the most of the years ahead of you? Research on successful aging points to three very clear lifestyle guideposts:

1. Connecting with others
2. Challenging oneself
3. Contributing to others

These lifestyle factors are of interest to those who want the last third of their life to be the most fruitful stage of all. If the goal is to strive for transcending dividends in this stage of life, it will lead to some pertinent life questions (which all have financial implications) such as:

- With whom are you most looking to make connections?
- How will you continue to challenge your intellect and faculties? (Alzheimer's research now demonstrates the accelerated decline of individuals who are not challenging themselves intellectually in their 50s and 60s)
- What causes are you hoping to assist?

This hypothetical query can launch another powerful dialogue: "Imagine you are now 90 years old. Looking back on the last 25 years, what have you accomplished for yourself? For others?"

A 70-year-old cancer survivor told us the story of going into the cancer clinic and observing the different mindsets of the people there. He shared, "I made some mental notes regarding the approach of the survival and surrender crowds. The surrender crowd was asking Why did this happen to me? and other such unanswerable questions. The survival crowd was goal-oriented and had things they still wanted to accomplish. That's where I fit, I had to get better, and I still had too much I wanted to get done." This man offers further evidence that life is not used up until a person decides that it is. The next generation of retirees is heaven-bent on making the most of their lives.

Conversations like this take the "tired" out of re*tired* and leave only the "re." That little prefix can mean a lot of things for the person who discovers the New Retirementality. It can mean regenerating, renewing, reinvigorating, or rediscovering. It means anything but resigning and reclining. Every vision of retired life is unique—it's your job to understand the life your clients want before beginning the process of helping them figure out how to pay for it.

C h a p t e r

14

BRING MEANING TO MY MONEY

The New Venture Philanthropy Dialogue

"We must perform a kind of Copernican revolution and give the question of the meaning of life an entirely new twist, to wit: It is life itself that asks questions of man. He should recognize that he is questioned, questioned by life; he has to respond by being responsible; and he can answer to life only by answering for his life."

Victor Frankl, *The Doctor and the Soul*

Alan knew that the gentleman sitting before him was hungry for a conversation beyond the numbers, benchmarks, and planning strategies. He had responded to Alan's advertising of "financial life planning" and the promise of a more meaningful dialogue around money. He spent a good 45 minutes talking about gaining financial satisfaction, achieving life balance, and developing a personal definition of true wealth.

The prospective client, after engaging in these discussions, commented, "This was the best discussion around money I have ever had, but," he added, "you need to know something about me regarding money. I'm not interested in making any more, although I would like to protect what I have from unnecessary taxes. What I would really like you to do," he challenged Alan, "is help me bring *meaning* to my money."

C h a p t e r

14

BRING MEANING TO MY MONEY

The New Venture Philanthropy Dialogue

"We must perform a kind of Copernican revolution and give the question of the meaning of life an entirely new twist, to wit: It is life itself that asks questions of man. He should recognize that he is questioned, questioned by life; he has to respond by being responsible; and he can answer to life only by answering for his life."

Victor Frankl, *The Doctor and the Soul*

Alan knew that the gentleman sitting before him was hungry for a conversation beyond the numbers, benchmarks, and planning strategies. He had responded to Alan's advertising of "financial life planning" and the promise of a more meaningful dialogue around money. He spent a good 45 minutes talking about gaining financial satisfaction, achieving life balance, and developing a personal definition of true wealth.

The prospective client, after engaging in these discussions, commented, "This was the best discussion around money I have ever had, but," he added, "you need to know something about me regarding money. I'm not interested in making any more, although I would like to protect what I have from unnecessary taxes. What I would really like you to do," he challenged Alan, "is help me bring *meaning* to my money."

156

In the course of their dialogue, this man mentioned several businesses he owned, which fueled Alan's curiosity, and so he asked the man, "How much money do you have?"

"$1.5 billion," was his answer.

BRING MEANING TO MY MONEY

As successful baby boomers ramp up the liquidation of businesses or transition to doing something more meaningful with their lives, we are going to see an escalating interest in what we would characterize as the Venture Philanthropy dialogue—a conversation about capitalizing (in a philanthropic sense) on clients' assets, tangible and intangible. Your business will move from amassing means to building meaning around the means.

This sentiment is growing and there are not enough advisors in the marketplace who can provide the conversation these people want to have. They are ready to transcend material collections, showpieces, and gain simply for the sake of gain. These individuals want to elevate their "game" to an altruistic level where they see the investment of their lives and wealth pay transcendent dividends.

PHILANTHROPY TRENDS

An article in *The Economist* predicted that another golden age of philanthropy is staged to begin in the United States and around the world. The article stated, "There are signs that a new kind of donor is emerging, with a new approach to giving. That new approach includes being more personally involved with their giving and placing a much higher premium on accountability."

According to Bruce Meyerson of the Associated Press in an article in *The Daily Star,* "While they may not have 26 billion [dollars] to sock away into a foundation like Bill Gates, many of his fellow baby boomers won't settle for just writing checks to their favorite charities."

With a first wave of boomers nearing retirement, and many starting to receive inheritance from their parents, a growing number are establishing family foundations with endowments as small as $50,000 to $100,000. According to Guidestar, nonprofit organizations are growing at an amazing and unprecedented rate. The wealth created in the 1990s has funded a virtual explosion of family foundations, charitable trusts, supporting organizations, and giving in general. In August 2002, there were 1.1 million nonprofits in the Guidestar database. By August 2004, the number was up to 1.9 million—an increase of 73 percent in just two years!

Boomers are opening accounts with community-based foundations and setting up "virtual" foundations with donor-advised funds which allow the individual to decide when, where, and how much to contribute. This idea fits the baby boom generation's approach to life, family, and personal fulfillment (they are figuring out that "giving while you're living" is a part of the fulfillment puzzle).

This generation is more hands-on with their giving than their parents were, opting for personal involvement, local charities, and often designing their own approaches for social involvement. According to the Indiana University Center on Philanthropy, the age group that is giving most is 50 to 65 years old—with some leveling out or slowing down at age 65. According to Melissa Berman of the Rockefeller Philanthropy Advisors, a nonprofit organization that provides planning and operational assistance to family foundations and charitable endeavors, "Many of the older boomers have reached a place in their lives where they have passed the immediate pressures of career building and raising kids to step back and say, 'What do I want to do with my time and resources?'"

Another sign is the growing popularity of community foundations (which numbered over 650 in 2002 with total assets of over

$3 billion) and the growing popularity of donor fund offerings by firms like Vanguard and Fidelity.

Research on the increase in family foundations by The Foundation Center reveals that the number of family foundations grew by over 60 percent between 1998 and 2002 to over 30,000 such foundations. It is worth noting that two-thirds of these family foundations had less than $1 million in assets when the foundations began. It is estimated that the number of American foundations may have doubled from 1990 to 2005.

According to FinancialCounsel.com there is a vast majority of middle income individuals who make annual gifts based on generosity rather than tax motives. Case in point: nonprofits feared an ebb in donations with the advent of the Economic Growth and Tax Relief Reconciliation Act (EGTRRA), which reduced top income tax rates. However, donations actually increased after that tax cut by over $1 billion, which demonstrates that this giving ethos is deeply rooted in the boomer generation.

BECOMING AN EYEWITNESS TO YOUR OWN GOODNESS

A watershed moment in the world of philanthropy came from Charles Feeney, cofounder of Duty Free Shoppers Group, Ltd, who sold his share of the business for $3.5 billion and proceeded to give away all but about $5 million of his personal fortune. His foundation, Atlantic Philanthropies, recently announced that it was going to quadruple its distribution of grants from $100 million to $400 million per year in order exhaust the entire endowment in 12 to 15 years! Why such charitable aggression? Feeney capsulated his approach with the now popular phrase he has been credited with coining: He is a believer in "giving while living."

Philanthropy once implied that the donor was dead; but now, it has been expanded to include living donors—and highly involved donors as well, with a bent for highly personalized giving. Individualized expression is the description that captures the boomer ethos. Should it surprise anyone that this group, which has created its own individualized career tracks and borne the responsibility of its own retirement, would foster an unprecedented age of highly personalized giving?

ADVENTURERS IN PHILANTHROPY

If you carefully examine the goals and ambitions of highly successful individuals as they phase out of corporate careers, you will find in the vast majority a desire to teach, mentor, help, develop, and create ways of touching lives with the skill sets they have gained in building successful businesses. They are ready to move from success to significance.

- Bill, a retired senior manager from a *Forbes* top 100 company, spent the last three years gaining his CFP so he could provide financial planning for single mothers who couldn't afford it.
- JoEllen, a successful publicist, is trimming her for-profit schedule to part time in order to have time to help selected charities with her skills and services.
- Joseph, an entrepreneur, is developing football camps throughout the summer as a medium for teaching important life values and is utilizing well-known college coaches and players as drawing cards to attract youth.
- John and Lucy, retired owners of an industry-leading company and heirs to a fortune in the mid-eight figures, spent their time searching out meaningful but struggling charities that were operating "under the radar" of public notoriety. They partnered with these charities financially and as members of their boards to solidify their causes.

Many venture philanthropists are joining forces with others who share their thirst for charity and accountability and are creating novel approaches to age-old problems in local and global settings. Many of these organizations take the "venture capital" business aspects of their approach very seriously by implementing quarterly controls and metrics and holding causes accountable for results.

The venture capital metaphor has been raised another degree by the Center for Venture Philanthropy (CVP), an offshoot of the Peninsula Community Foundation in San Mateo, California (located in the heart of Venture Capital, U.S.A). The center recently published a paper entitled "Five Key Elements of Venture Philanthropy and Five Years of Documented Results." The five elements they promote reveal the clear venture capital analogy:

1. *Investment as a long-term plan for social change.* Comprehensive plans for social change start with an audacious goal and an action plan to achieve it.
2. *Managing partner relationships.* All ground rules are set, including written agreements that define the roles and responsibilities of the participants: nonprofit leaders, investors, and CVP fund managers,
3. *Accountability-for-results process.* This rigorous methodology holds participants accountable and delivers measurable results on a quarterly basis.
4. *Provision of cash and expertise.* CVP provides cash and critical expertise—subject matter specialists, investor forums, and evaluation expertise—all necessary to tackle the biggest social issues.
5. *An exit strategy.* Create a unique exit strategy for each fund, making possible shared responsibility for sustained change.

Here are some examples of this brand of venture philanthropy ethos at work in America with consequences felt around the world.

- *Austin Social Venture Partners* (Austin, Texas) provide financial support and business expertise to help its nonprofit "investees" develop more efficient, sustainable organizations. Their strategy is to address root causes of community problems.
- *Global Partnerships* (Seattle, Washington) raise private sector funds to support village banking and microcredit programs in Central and South America.
- *New Profit, Inc.* (Boston, Massachusetts) seeks to attract new financial and intellectual capital to the nonprofit sector and is working on developing new financing mechanisms for investing in social entrepreneurs.
- *The Acumen Fund* (http://www.acumenfund.org) is a venture philanthropy fund that was seeded with capital from the Rockefeller Foundation and Cisco Systems Foundation, and working in conjunction with three individual philanthropists. The Acumen Fund is focused on the four billion inhabits of our planet living on less than $4 per day and provides solutions as practical as netted bedding for tens of thousands of people at high risk for malaria because of exposure to disease-carrying insects.

There are scores of other groups addressing job creation and affordable housing, creating opportunities in disenfranchised communities, and serving innumerable other needs in the world.

CFOS FOR THE NEW VPS

These stories are endless and yet have just begun to be told in our world. We are entering an age of "signature charity," where benefactors are seeking to leave a unique and indelible fingerprint in causes that have moved their heart. Instead of sending big checks to big charities, the entrepreneurial spirit is driving these individuals to do something different. Which financial professionals or firms will come alongside this wave of compassionate capitalism?

For those who want to ride a meaningful and prosperous wave into the future, we would suggest the examination of the venture philanthropy trend. It is interesting to note that when Mitch wrote the first edition of his book *The New Retirementality* and suggested the term *venture philanthropy*, he could find no Internet references to the term. Five years later, there are scores of people and groups rallying around the idea. This is not to imply that the book had anything to do with popularizing the term, but instead that the marriage of the words, *venture* and *philanthropy* feels instinctive and rings intuitively for this generation.

We are using the term *venture philanthropy* in a much broader sense than the venture capitalist crowd. We are including the free agents, entrepreneurs, and business owners who are contemplating cashing out or spreading their entrepreneurial instincts toward charity. What is venture philanthropy? It is the utilization of all resources, tangible and intangible, that your clients can bring to bear in the process of actualizing their own philanthropic instincts.

This is a market that will see tremendous growth and reward the tuned-in and purpose-driven advisor with manifold opportunities.

The idea behind the venture philanthropy dialogue is to help clients flesh out:

- The roots of their philanthropic sentiments
- The causes that most interest them
- The specialized insights, skills, and visions they have to offer
- The ultimate good their money can do

QUESTIONS TO ASK

What people or causes have made an impact in your life and in the lives of those you love? What we are really asking here is,

"Who has helped you along the way?" or, maybe even, "Who do you wish had been there along the way?"

Whether someone was there or not, those associations are indelibly printed in our memory banks and are often at the root of the philanthropic instinct. "Someone was there for me when I really needed help. I want to be there for others," or, "My father always wanted to be an engineer, but he was too poor and worked common labor his whole life. He always wished his life had turned out differently. I want to help people in that sort of situation."

This is a conversation that is pregnant with possibilities for setting up scholarship funds and specialty foundations. Explore the possibilities and encourage the idea of doing something unique.

Do you have any ideas for a cause or charity that you think could fill an important need in our world? Perhaps you have clients like George and Darrell Thompson, a father and son who share philanthropic pulses. Upon being offered early retirement as a senior level manager at IBM, George decided to follow his heart with his money, energy, and time. He had always been bothered by racial intolerance in his community and decided to do something about it. He founded prejudice reduction workshops for The Diversity Council and designed programs for school children and the workplace promoting tolerance and understanding. The program reaches tens of thousands yearly.

George's son Darrell was looking for something significant to do with his talents and energy after retiring from the NFL. He found his life's work with the Bolder Options program, which mentors inner-city youth who have lacked a positive male role model in their lives and have begun to show signs of taking the wrong path. They use biking and running as a forum for building significant relationships and helping change the lives of these youth.

How do you know that the clients sitting before you do not harbor these sorts of philanthropic dreams? You won't know until you ask. Chances are they will also lead you to others just like them.

What do you have to offer other than your money to help further the causes you believe in? Some years back Mitch's step-mother, Muriel, was undergoing treatment for small cell lymphoma and traveling cross-country to the Mayo Clinic four to six times per year for treatment. Mitch saw firsthand how taxing the experience was on both her and his father—financially as well as physically and psychologically. The cost of chemotherapy is dear, and it is expensive to fly across the country. Mitch could also observe the added stress the financial issues were bringing to the situation and understood the detrimental effect such stress could produce on the immune system.

Being a frequent flyer he saw an easy and painless solution: he gave Muriel his "World Perks" account information and let her be her own travel agent with the miles. Muriel and Mitch's dad constantly remarked about the reduced stress and joy of not having to worry about coming up with the funds to get treatment. It was that easy, simply transferring a resource that could serve one party better than another. The last thing Mitch wanted to do after accumulating all those miles was to go on another trip, and so the miles simply stacked up.

A couple of years ago, Mitch happened to mention the idea of actually developing a program like this with the Mayo Clinic, and they agreed that it would be beneficial to many of their patients. Not long after that the American Cancer Society became involved in the conversation and The Rxtra Mile Program was born (see the Appendix). This program encourages frequent fliers to donate their miles to help cancer patients get to and from the Mayo Clinic (or another clinic if they prefer).

There is no telling the breadth and reach of the charitable ideas that can and will be born just by asking this question. Many people have made observations about underserved needs and unjust and inequitable circumstances but could use just a little nudge of encouragement to actually do something about it. That nudge come could from you in this conversation.

What do you feel is the greatest good that can come from your wealth? Brooks Moneypenny, a successful financial advisor with Morgan-Keegan, believes that the greatest good that can come from his wealth is to teach his children the joy and fulfillment that can come from a life of helping those less fortunate. He decided that he would begin to teach his children (while they are young) about this connection to meaningful money and purposeful living by setting up donor-advised funds in each of the children's names. Each year the children now have the joyous task of finding a cause that they really care about and making a gift to an approved charity. They not only are learning to give, but they also are learning to live with their eyes wide open to the needs of others and to the possibilities of making a difference.

Well done, Brooks! Our compliments, and may a million clients and ten thousand advisors follow your insightful example.

THE SIGNATURE STATEMENT OF WEALTH

We could use our money to buy the fanciest car in the world but somebody has already done that. We could build a mansion that rises like a castle to the sky but there will always be a bigger, better, more amazing home than the one we build. People are looking to build something that hands and rust and decay cannot destroy. They seek an eternal container for their best selves, a vehicle for leaving their unique signature upon this planet. This container of dreams and inspiration is the result of the philanthropic pulse and charitable effort. We can do better than writing checks for tax purposes. We can invest our hearts, the sum of our experiences, and our material gain, and leave a truly meaningful mark on this world—a signature that seals who we are and what matters most to us.

This is the harvest of the venture philanthropy dialogue.

15

THE MATURE DIALOGUE

"I'm not an old man. I'm a middle-aged man living in an older wrapper. I know I
may look old to you but don't talk to me like I am. Talk to me like you would anyone
else. I'm simply a human being with the advantages of experience."

77-year-old client

"Has he any reason to envy the young people that he sees, or wax nostalgic for his own
youth? What reason has he to envy a young person? For the possibilities that young
person has, the future that is in store for him? 'No, thank you,' he will think. 'Instead of
possibilities, I have realities in my past—not only the reality of work done and of love
loved, but of suffering suffered. These are the things of which I am most proud.'"

Victor Frankl

How does your dialogue evolve as your client matures? Brain science has established the fact that there is a substantial shift toward right-brain orientation as people move past the age of 60. How does this shift impact your relationships and your business?

A study by the Lincoln Long Life Institute echoes many of the themes that surfaced in our research and dialogues into the mature dialogue and the sort of conversation that would resonate with those in the third-ager class. The study spotlighted the following issues:

- Successful 70-year-olds found that controlling their finances throughout their lengthy retirement has proved to be more complicated than they envisioned. Fifty-four percent had never thought about how long they would spend in retirement. Another 43 percent had estimated retirement to last 22 years. Research, however, demonstrates that people need to plan on 25 to 35 years.

- Most successful 70-year-olds link their happiness to the ability to be independent (94 percent say it is a major source of satisfaction, followed by housing, health, financial situation, and time spent with children).

- Affluent respondents were twice as likely to have never stopped working. They are three times as likely to work as their peers. They work because they like the intellectual stimulation, social aspects of the job, and enjoy what they do.

- In regard to legacy, they are decidedly focused on enjoying the fruits of their labor during their retirement years and view leaving an inheritance as a lower priority (possibly because their kids don't need it). Only 46 percent say leaving an inheritance is important.

- The study suggested that it is imperative to them to be self-reliant so that they don't end up being financial burdens to their relatives, and in return they seemed to expect their adult children to adopt similar values and achieve financial success on their own.

- They are most generous with advice—80 percent reported offering financial advice to their children even though only 15 percent reported receiving retirement advice from their parents.

- Affluent clients are looking for life insurance and investment products that can meet their long-term retirement needs, providing flexibility, upside growth potential, and assurances that their investments will remain safe over time.

CLOSE TO HOME

Before writing this chapter we decided to go to the best resources we could find on what would make for an intriguing and compelling dialogue with your more mature clients, or the third-agers, as they are beginning to be called. These are not baby boomers; these are the people that spawned the boom. Born between 1930 and 1945, these individuals have quietly gone about making substantive shifts in how one lives after retirement (a trend for which baby boomers want to take credit—although a boomer has yet to turn 65!).

These people have quietly amended the aging bill of rights and what it takes to achieve "life, liberty, and the pursuit of happiness." We decided to interview some informed sources from this generational cohort—two of which are our fathers, Bob West and Tom Anthony. Following are some of the summations and pithy commentary from calls and meetings we had with representatives of the third-agers to discuss the mature dialogue. Three of the questions we asked were:

1. What are your greatest concerns going forward?
2. How have you seen retirement change as a lifestyle?
3. What are you looking for in an advisor?

Question 1: What are your greatest concerns going forward?

Health Care and Inflation

- "I'm concerned about being able to pay the ever-rising costs of health care, especially as my money becomes worth less each and every year because of inflation."
- "I'm doing everything I can with my dieting, exercising, and controlling stress to help keep my health from being an issue. I understand that you can't control everything, but

I'm addressing the parts I can control because I know that poor health is the greatest killer of wealth."

Ability to Generate Income

- "I'm concerned about being able to generate some income in case the income I have proves to be too little to meet my needs down the road."
- "I work part time now just to keep myself current in the workplace. I don't really need the extra income so I'm saving it against a day where I may need it."
- "I really can use the extra income I'm making, but I am also glad to be out working 20 hours a week. I enjoy the stimulation of being around younger people and contributing."

If I Live to Be 95

- "Frankly, I don't know what I'll do if I do live to be 95. It's a bit disconcerting to think about being 23 years older than I am now with less to support me and even less ability to earn any more."
- "My needs are quite simple now and will be even simpler then. Most important to me would be having my faculties intact and possessing the ability to enjoy the fact that I am still around. I see a lot of people at 95 today living good, fruitful days."

Rising Taxes and Utilities

- "It seems like the taxes keep going up, the utilities keep going up, the cost of travel keeps going up, all our overhead keeps going up, but we're standing still."
- "When you think about what things cost 30 years ago, like a gallon of gas or milk, and the chance that they'll go up that

much in the next 30 years makes you glad that you probably won't be consuming as much."

- "It really makes me glad that I saved as much as I did when I see how costs keep going up. In some ways it makes me feel like I could never have enough. I used to think that if I had $2 million socked away I'd never have to think about it again. Now I wonder."

Passing on What I've Gathered

- "I remember when my father was getting older we tried to talk to him and our mother about moving the family farm into some sort of trust to protect it against the enormous costs of living in a senior citizen home. He was pretty stubborn and wouldn't hear of it at the time, being pretty healthy and vigorous in his early 80s. Then in his 90s he slipped and the $5,000 a month ate away at everything until nothing was left. I don't want to see something like that happen to me and my children."
- "My children really don't need anything from me, they are all doing quite well, but I will leave them something for memory's sake I'm sure. I would like to find a way to continue our family legacy and heritage by leaving them my stories to pass on to their children."

Not Being a Burden to My Children

- "I worry about being a burden to my children. I don't want them to have to have their life consumed with taking care of me and resenting it."
- "In my day we had Grandpa or Grandma living with us when they got along in years—it was just the way we lived. Our daughter and husband have already brought this idea up to us in our mid-70s and they are planning to get a large one-story home with two separate living quarters. They insisted

on this and helped us to get over our concerns about being a burden to them."

Asset Rich and Cash Poor

- "The thing that concerns me is that on paper I look pretty good but I can't do a whole lot with it. For example, I bought this house on a golf course when I retired for about $200,000 and it's worth $450,000 now. But what good does that do me? It actually is working against me because my taxes are now double and my other costs are going up as well. I can't spend any of that wealth because it's not 'real' money to me and I don't want to get more of a house because we just couldn't get the trade-off we would need."
- "It's ironic to listen to my kids talk about how great the low rates on lending are, and I'm happy for what they have been able to get with those low rates, but those low rates don't help those of us whose assets are fixed. Boy, wouldn't I love to see some of those high rates from the early '80s. I'd be living on easy street with those!"
- "It's frustrating to be sitting on net worth that doesn't translate to quality of living. I know people who have started with the reverse mortgage, but then I wonder what happens if you outlive even that? Where do you go then?"

Question 2: How have you seen retirement change as a lifestyle?

Lifestyles Today Are More Active

- "I see so many people my age working out at the health club, going on lots of trips and adventures, and doing strenuous activities on those trips that you would never have seen years ago. A lot of today's 70-somethings are acting like 50-somethings and enjoying everything they can."

Authors' Note: Many of the concerns we heard expressed are rooted in the double-edged reality of living on a fixed income with unpredictable inflationary factors. It is also apparent that there is a dark underbelly to what many of us would consider "good" economic news, such as low borrowing rates, which translates into less income for them. For many, the psychological state is like building a fairly high retirement tower and then standing out and watching the water rise year after year and wondering, "How long will I be safe here?"

The following chart, published by the U.S. Department of Commerce and Bureau of Economic Analysis, indicates where these concerns may be coming from—their memory bank. They can remember the cost of things 30 to 50 years ago, and the prospect of what those things are costing now (and will cost in the future) can cause anxiety and insecurity. (Note: Although this is an older study, it is an excellent indicator of inflationary trends over a 50-year period.)

Retirement Expenses	1949	1999
Food, tobacco, and alcohol	33%	15%
Household operation	15	11
Clothing and accessories	14	6
Transportation	11	11
Housing	10	15
Recreation	6	8
Medical care	5	18

- "I'm planning a life on the go. I don't see myself slowing down or cutting back that much. I worry a little bit about being able to afford to do all the things I want to do, like traveling overseas, playing great golf courses, and visiting my kids and grandkids."
- "I think you have to have something new and exciting to look forward to or you'll get bored and negative. I'm always thinking of new things I want to do, new things I can learn, places I want to go."

- "It used to be that when you retired you sat at the café and played cards or sat out on the bench and watched people drive by. There's no place in my life for a life like that. I want to do things that make me feel useful."

Some People Can't Retire

- "I have a friend who worked for 30 years for the airlines and looked forward to a great pension—only to be stuck with the realization that she'll get about half of what she thought. She is going to have to do something to make up the difference."
- "I know some people who are working at Wal-Mart or the grocery store and need the money, but say they are glad they are doing it. It keeps them fresh and in circulation. They say they would do it even if they didn't need the money."
- "I know a lot of people who can't retire, not just for economic reasons but for sanity reasons. They have too much energy, get bored too easily, and just want the excitement of having something to look forward to each day. 'Slowing down' isn't in their vocabulary. If they sat around they would rot away quickly. Now that we've potentially got 30-year retirements, people are beginning to pay more attention to how much retirement they can take."

Some Veterans Are Being Hired Back Part Time by Companies and Others Are Working Well into Their 70s

- "One of the things I am most thankful for is that as a professional who makes my own career decisions [as a financial advisor], I don't have a company telling me when I'm finished. I have developed a wonderful business with clientele I enjoy, and I love what I do. I can't find a good reason to quit—especially after witnessing what has happened to many of my retired clients who were so aimless upon retirement. I can't think of one good reason to quit something I love doing and that brings so much value. I'm going to do it until

I'm no longer competent. Look at [Federal Reserve Board chairman Alan] Greenspan's tenure. His experience was an asset not a liability."

- "I've seen many people go back and work out deals with their former employers on a part-time consulting basis and from what I can see, they like the current arrangement a lot better than the former. They work shorter hours but are still involved with projects that challenge them."
- "Some people are going back part time and dedicating the earnings to paying for their health care or travel or some other cost of living. This helps keep a good margin of comfort."

There's a Changed Focus

- "I've seen the focus change for many people, including myself, from what I can get [six rounds of golf a week] to what I can give. Getting up with nothing but a tee time doesn't do it for me. I need to know I'm making a difference during the week as well as know that I'm enjoying myself."
- "Just living for the sake of loving money can kill you. If all you do is work for money and ignore the other important areas of life in the process just to retire, you're going to find a shallow life."
- "I really want to find ways to share my experiences and skills to help others. That's the richest payoff of all, don't you think? It's also very important to me to be in a good enough financial position to be able to help others."
- "Philanthropy is more personal and more involved these days. I want to be personally involved by meeting the people I'm helping and seeing the good I am doing. It's not just about writing a check—although that may be a part of it."
- "A lot of us have discovered that the prime requisites for a happy life are meaningful work and relationships. I've seen what happens when people isolate themselves, and it's not good. Maintaining our independence is all-important."

Authors' Note: Read between the lines and you can see that there is ample opportunity for the advisor that is in touch with the lifestyle of new retirees. They have plans, hopes, and aspirations for the years ahead and will need good financial planning to see these ideas come to fruition. Philanthropic aspirations are a growing sentiment with this group and well worth venturing a dialogue.

Question 3: What are you looking for in an advisor?"

Get to Know Me

- "I want an advisor who doesn't look like he wants to make a sale, asks a lot of questions, and gets to know who I am."
- "Listen 65 percent of the time and talk 35 percent. I've met many financial professionals who do not take enough time to get to know me and seemed intent on just 'getting the order.' I need to see that you have an interest in helping me."
- "I look for sincerity. Do I get the feeling that they really care and want to make a difference?"
- "I want to work with someone who makes a real effort at staying in touch and gets to know me. I also want them to be proactive when there is bad news and initiate a conversation with me."

Know Your Stuff

- "I like to talk to someone who has a lot of knowledge about a number of products and ideas. I also want someone with a wide range of clients—and I want to talk to some of those clients."
- "Just like when I buy a car I don't want to talk to some rookie who doesn't know the first thing about the vehicle I want, neither do I want to deal with someone on investments who

only knows about a couple of things. Before I landed with my planner I was at a bank where all this young guy did was try to sell me an annuity. My planner went through all the ins and outs and showed me the ups and downs of every type of investment and then let me make my decision."

My Money Is Sacred Turf

- "Don't rush me. My life is tied to this decision. The last thing I need to feel is hurried."
- "I know I'm not alone when I say I have concerns about integrity. I see all these ads on TV, but nothing seems to resonate from these ads. Are they saying all these things because they know that a lot of us don't trust them anymore?"
- "I worry about making a mistake because at this stage it could be so costly. If I lose too much of what I have, I can't just go out and make it again like some young guy. This is it for me. The quality of my life hinges on these financial decisions."
- "I want to know that the company I'm doing business with is playing by the rules and is secure. What's the point of buying insurance products if the company isn't going to be around to pay off on them? When you read about big com-

Authors' Note: Caring, competence, and integrity were the watchwords for what the experienced set is looking for in a relationship with their financial advisor. One comment that surprised us was this, "I prefer working with younger advisors because they have more energy, work harder, and try harder to find new ideas. I just want to see enthusiasm for the right reasons." So we conclude that there is plenty of room for the younger advisor with the experienced crowd if they demonstrate the proper mores, knowledge, and passion for helping their clients.

panies going under it makes you think twice about whom
you work with."

- "I like people who appreciate what it took for me to get where
I am and apply that level of respect regarding their suggestions. I'm not at a place where I want to take big risks."

RELATE AND EDUCATE

In an article in *Registered Representative,* Louis Harvey, president of Dalbar, a financial services research firm in Boston, states,
"I cannot stress the importance of communication strongly enough.
The number one reason an investor will leave a broker is that the
client's expectations were not met and/or communicated clearly."
While good communication alone cannot sustain a relationship,
poor communication will nearly always break it.

Harvey offers an example of a client transferring funds from
his current advisor at a major wire house to a managed money account with another advisor. "The client did this because he was
not aware that his existing advisor offered these same services. By
the time the first advisor found out, it was too late. The first advisor didn't even know that the assets he had from the client were
only a small portion of the client's net worth," Harvey adds.

According to a J.D. Power and Associates survey, the job you
do educating your clients and the level of service you provide are
truly pivotal factors in investor satisfaction.

"Investors want information and education," says Nancy Salk,
director of research for J.D. Power and Associates in Agoura Hills,
California. "With greater access to a plethora of financial material
from the Internet and media, investors are in information overload."

According to research by NFO World Group, in the affluent
market, educational and relational issues come to the fore as well.
Today's affluent customer demands a combination of five critical
capabilities to retain their loyalty and trust:

1. Investment performance
2. Quality service
3. Knowledgeable representatives and advisors
4. Ability to resolve problems
5. Familiarity with their specific situation

According to a study by the Spectrum Group, 83 percent of pentamillionaire households expect their advisor to understand their total financial picture. Eighty-four percent indicated that they would always want a personal relationship with a financial advisor.

The amount of money seems to be beside the point when it comes to the client's story. When a client says, "I want you to be familiar with my specific situation," they are really saying, "I want you to know my story."

These client satisfaction issues are especially relevant with the mature crowd, many of whom may become confused with too much jargon, data, and seemingly conflicting information. They were telling us that they want context and education and an advisor who reaches out.

PEOPLE, NOT OLD PEOPLE

One final note on engaging in meaningful dialogues with your mature clients regards not what you talk about but *how* you talk about it. According to studies on communicating with the mature, many older clients feel they are talked to in stereotypical modes of conversation.

One study by the Intergenerational Communication Across the Life Span demonstrated that "not only are older speakers perceived in stereotyped ways but the content of their talk is often interpreted stereotypically. By drawing on rules or stereotypes to decide what topics are appropriate for intergenerational talk, people may constrain and limit possibilities for relational development."

Research from this study demonstrated both the negative and positive stereotypes often reinforced in conversations with mature clients.

Negative Stereotypes	Positive Stereotypes
Severely impaired	Perfect grandparents
Recluse	"John Wayne" conservative
Shrew/curmudgeon	Golden-ager
Despondent	

Students of our fanatical curiosity and biographers approach will naturally avoid pigeonholing mature clients, or any other client for that matter, into any preconceived notion of what "people their age" ought to be like. One study on the patronizing of matures (the "deary" syndrome) by researchers Angie Williams and Virpi Ylanne concluded, "Our research is populated by elders who are patronized, treated benignly as sweet little old dears, or more negatively as helpless and decrepit, or as struggling heroically with the rigors of ill health and decrement."

As one gentleman in his 80s put it when asked what he would advise to those seeking meaningful dialogue with him, "Don't be fooled by what you see. I can't see or hear as well as I once did, but I can see what you're up to and hear what you really mean when you talk to me. I may look like an old man to you, but I'm an experienced man to me—a guy with a lot of miles and stories to tell. Don't ever get so distracted by this older person sitting in front of you that you forget that he is a person."

We can't say it any better than he did. They are the matures—and that means they know more because they have seen and experienced more. All the more reason to commence meaningful conversations, hold your tongue, and absorb the stories they tell. Our next chapter will deal with what might be the most meaningful conversation you will ever have with a client, the legacy dialogue.

16

I REMEMBER YOU

Engaging in the Legacy Dialogue

"Every time an older person dies a museum closes."

Kofi Annan, Secretary General of the United Nations

Brett was just a green attorney, fresh out of law school when his father, a respected financial advisor, brought a client in to see him regarding an estate planning issue. His father, who was a master of understanding the emotional side of the business, brought this client to him partly as a learning experience. It seemed that his father's client was quite angry with a son's behavior and character and wanted to write him out of the will.

Brett recalls how his father cringed when he informed the frustrated and angry client that there are a lot of countries—those in Europe for example—where it's not legal to disinherit your child, but in America it is perfectly OK. Brett went on to share what he knew about estate law in Europe and America. He then reminded the client of the irrevocable nature of such a decision and went on to give a full explanation of legal options.

When he was finished, Brett picked up from the client's body language that he didn't appreciate the lesson in European law.

Brett's father picked up on the signals as well and asked Brett if he wouldn't mind leaving the conference room for a bit.

After the client left, his father gave Brett an invaluable object lesson on what really matters in legacy work—and it wasn't the technical details, as important as they can be. He told Brett that he simply asked his client, "How do you want to be remembered?" This question helped to unlock the client's anger and confusion about what to do. He realized that, no matter how badly his son had behaved, he didn't want to be remembered as a father who rejected him, even from the grave. A more graceful compromise was found—keep the son in the will with some "spendthrift" provisions.

Because of the wisdom of Brett's father, the client walked away with a plan for his estate and for his heart, which is at the very center of what estate planning was meant to be (before tax planners took over the process)—a posthumous, material expression of the heart.

The contrast in this story was a young, educated professional trying to utilize his knowledge, and another man, more seasoned in the art of human relationships, sharing his experience and emotional insights. Brett took his father's intuitive approach to heart and currently utilizes these insights each and every day in his work as the field director of advanced sales for Nationwide. This specialized position takes him into a constant stream of casework where he is helping advisors help families leave a better quality legacy.

Having grown up around an insightful financial advisor and being trained in legal issues, Brett brings a unique perspective to the cases he touches. He finds that he still has to wrestle with the overly technical tendencies that many advisors use to approach estate planning. Many will tell him they "just want the facts," and Brett will respond that these are the facts—the soft facts. In estate planning no facts are more important.

His passion is to teach advisors and others working on estate planning the questions that don't get asked, but should be. He laments that there persists out there a shortsighted and monomaniacal emphasis on tax planning as the core of estate planning.

Brett's point is well taken. Here again we see a financial services monologue at work dealing with a peripheral issue (tax efficiency) as if it were the core issue. This obsession with the technical tends to put the heart of the matter (a personal legacy) in the supporting role and puts Uncle Sam and his tax codes in the lead, thereby missing a tremendous opportunity for both service and cementing a broad family relationship. We believe that as an industry, we can do much better with this particular issue by stepping up the context and quality of the dialogue around estate planning.

In her article, "Values Based Planning," Kris Arnzen outlines these questions.

- How do you want to be remembered?
- How was your wealth created?
- How will you pass on your wisdom as well as your wealth?
- Do you want to leave a societal legacy?
- What is the most important thing you want to accomplish in your life?

Clearly there is a need for a more balanced left-brain/right-brain approach to this critical aspect of financial services. As we demonstrated in our earlier book, *StorySelling for Financial Advisors,* the lion's share of communication technique employed in financial services is weighted to the number crunching, logic-grinding left brain and largely ignores a tropical storm of dissatisfied emotion and contextual curiosity. Gerald M. Condon's *Beyond the Grave: The Right Way and the Wrong Way of Leaving Money to Your Children (and Others)* is a book that attempts to take more balanced left-brain/right-brain approach to this topic.

Most books on estate planning explain how to maximize inheritance, minimize taxes, avoid probate, set up trusts, and other technical and tactical details. The Condons, a father and son lawyer team, do this as well, but what they also do is consider the psychological and emotional aspects of leaving and inheriting money. The Condons cover such possibilities as "protecting" the inheritance from one's child or spouse, preventing squabbles over inherited property, selecting trustees or guardians, avoiding the disputes between second spouses and children of first marriages, leaving money for pets, etc. These authors provide a thorough look at inheritance planning with an eye toward maintaining good, stable family relations well after the estate has been settled.

For the sake of establishing context and priorities in the estate planning process you might want to use a tool like the following Well-th Transfer Priority Chart™ created by the Financial Life Planning Institute (see Figure 16.1). The institute's first suggestion for initiating conversations around estate planning is to call it something besides "estate planning."

For many people the term conjures up images of rich people in mansions—a process for people like Thurston Howell, III, not me, after all, I don't really have an "estate." The institute suggests the term *well-th transfer* because it places the emphasis on being well when the process is finished, as opposed to the more common and narrow goal of being "tax efficient."

WELL-TH TRANSFER PRIORITY CHART

This sort of process helps to place the tax issue in its proper context and enables clients to see the big picture—much of which is emotional in nature, as it applies to their estate plan.

If a client places a high priority on number 7, transferring his or her history, experiences, and life lessons to heirs, you may want to utilize the full Memory Bank™ system, which was created for the purpose of capturing and transferring the stories that make up the essence of your client's life. The Memory Bank system gives your client a biographical template for interviewing loved ones.

FIGURE 16.1 *The Well-th Transfer Priority Chart*™

Directions: Rank your priorities by placing the numbers of the two highest priorities in the center heart. Place the numbers of the next four highest priorities in the black circle, and the numbers of the final four priorities in the outer gray circle.

1. Heirs understanding the values and principles that produced your wealth
2. Keeping the peace among family members after you are gone
3. Minimizing taxation to your assets.
4. Dividing the assets fairly and equitably
5. Reducing the negative impact of sudden wealth on your children and recipients
6. Ensuring that your legacy lives for generations (foundation or scholarships, etc.)
7. Transferring your history, experiences, and life lessons to your heirs
8. Investing in the perpetuation and well-being of your choice charities
9. Creating a scholarship for a specific type of person or predicament
10. Not leaving your children with unnecessary burdens after your passing

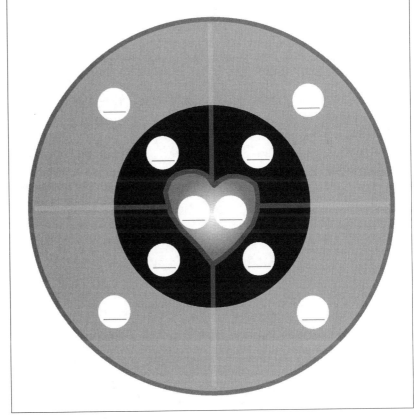

© 2005 Mitch Anthony

The interview is recorded on audio and then transcribed and edited into the finished product—an attractive and invaluable life narrative. Many estate planners offer this as a value-added service for their prized clients. What greater connection could you make with clients than to act as the medium for transferring the rich stories that constitute the life of someone they love?

Memorybank.org is an organization dedicated to helping people capture and transfer their histories, meaningful events, and lessons from life. They supply biographical templates and recommend recording devices (MP3 or video). Once the stories are captured, Memorybank.org then helps develop edited narratives, hard-bound books with pictures, audio CDs, and videos to pass on to loved ones.

Following are some sample topics from the Memorybank.org on the subject of recollections on work, wealth, and wisdom.

- What you learned about money when you were growing up
- Memorable incident(s) involving money that impacted your life when you were growing up
- Your first experiences with earning money
- Important lessons you have learned about earning money
- Your financial journey (highlights, lowlights, and reflections)
- The best money decisions you have made
- Some mistakes you made along the way
- What you have learned about the liberties and limitations of money (what money can and cannot do)
- The lasting legacy you want to leave regarding work and money

You will be amazed to read your clients' responses when you ask them to recall an incident involving money that impacted their lives when they were growing up. One client wrote that money was really tight in the small Texas town where he grew up and his family was dirt poor. His mother controlled the money in their household and gave her husband an allowance every week that amounted to enough to play nine holes of golf on the municipal course and buy a week's worth of chewing tobacco. The client, at age 11, caddied to earn money. One day he carried double bags for two rounds and made more in that one day than his father made in a week. He realized immediately that he had more control over his life than his father did.

We are of the opinion that the richest legacies your clients can leave are the stories that helped shape their lives. Their personal novels are eminently more interesting, dramatic, and relevant to their loved ones than any fiction selection on the *New York Times* bestseller list. We simply need to do a better job capturing and transferring these stories.

A FAMILY AFFAIR

"All happy families resemble one another, but each unhappy family is unhappy in its own way."

Leo Tolstoy, *Anna Karenina*

According to the Gallup Organization and other studies, there is going to be a great need for succession planning in family-owned businesses. Consider that:

- In the next ten years, succession will occur in over 50 percent of family businesses.
- Only 30 percent of businesses survive beyond the first generation.
- Only 57 percent have done any estate planning.
- Only 28 percent have a buy-sell agreement.
- Only 7 percent have advisors to help them with family relationship problems.

Carolyn Lloyd-Cohen, CLU, ChFC, AEP, of Lloyd-Cohen Associates in Clifton, New Jersey, offers this commentary on the family business: "On the one hand, there is the family. On the other hand, they have a business. It's impossible to totally separate the two. Just the admission of that is important. When it comes to what's good for the family or good for the business, it doesn't have to be an either/or situation. Maybe there's a compromise that will work."

The first problem in many cases is that the founder hasn't talked to the children to give them an idea of when they will gain control of the business. The second most common problem is that the parents don't turn over responsibility to the next generation early enough so that the children can build their own expertise to run the business. Another problematic dynamic that causes a rift in families is when one child is involved in the family business and the other isn't. Experienced planners and advisors indicate that initial conversations should focus on whether the client wants the nonparticipating child to participate in the business's growth and profitability. Most often clients agree that dividing the business equally in this situation isn't fair, and so planners often need to construct ways to leave uninvolved children other assets. As one veteran planner put it, "The worst thing to do is assume that the kids are going to figure it out on their own. That is a recipe for future disaster."

A recent article on estate planning offered an example of clients who had a son and daughter-in-law who were physicians. They also had a daughter who was a reporter and a son-in-law who was a librarian. They were all great people but in very different socioeconomic situations. The clients wanted to treat their children equally, but they were concerned about whether that was fair. Their advisor's solution was to bypass the children and set up appropriate trusts to fund the grandchildren's education. By doing so the parents reassured both children of their intentions to be fair and equal. These are the sorts of creative solutions that can result from dealing with the "softer facts" and core questions of estate planning such as:

- What solutions would be fairest to all involved?
- How can we make this transfer with the least possibility for strife and resentment?

Great estate planning or "well-th transfer" comes down to the quality of the communication process employed and how well that process integrates the emotional issues related to the estate and family.

In order to facilitate communication between clients and their heirs, Paula F. de Vos, CFP, president of Synergist Wealth Advisors LLC in Carmel, California, advocates values-based estate planning where the focus goes beyond tax-effective planning into intergenerational communication. This communication between family members forms a foundation for "opportunities not only for furthering the wishes and objectives of the first generation, but providing the ability and means to develop comprehensive 'family objectives' that are achieved across multigenerations."

With a firm that specializes in meeting the needs of families, including coordinating efforts among all advisors, de Vos believes that with family meetings, there is less opportunity for disagreement later on and stresses the importance of addressing issues early. "Friction in families can last 100 years or more. With the right resources in the right environment, if there is disagreement, there's an open forum to discuss issues without animosity." She also notes that in addition to assisting other advisors and clients in conducting successful family meetings, she helps with weekend-long retreats or drafting a "family wealth letter of intent" as a way of passing on a family's personal history and values.

Other experienced estate planners believe that the root of many estate conflicts is that heirs often have a sense of entitlement and expectation. They suggest that planners could avoid future conflicts by talking to younger clients to help them teach self-reliance and responsibility to their children. These qualities are best taught by the parents, instead of later, in the heat of emotion, by a planner or fiduciary.

In his book, *Becoming a Wealth Transfer Specialist,* Karl Bareither's work on communicating with family businesses on legacy issues may be the most impressive of all. He has created the FBR (Family & Business Renewal) System (http://www.fbrsystem.com) where he has designed an approach that helps advisors become experts at the left-brain/right-brain approach in communicating with family businesses and accomplishing successful legacy planning from both a technical and well-being perspective.

Bareither has designed a dialogue for family meetings and retreats that fleshes out a win-win solution for all involved. He learned early in his career that without a disciplined, holistic process, family communication fell to the worst common denominator. Following is a summary of the principles of Bareither's approach that he has been practicing successfully for over 30 years:

1. It's a family affair not just an owner's affair.
2. It's a process not a transaction.
3. It's an open agenda, not closed and secretive.
4. It's an asking format, not a telling one.
5. It enhances family life inclusion, not exclusion.
6. It's a way to open family dialogue, not close discussions.
7. The greatest resource is people, not equipment, product, or real estate.
8. It deals with both the external and the internal.
9. It helps to examine a time for change instead of just following what has always been.
10. It seeks input from family advisors instead of excluding anyone who might differ.
11. It uses an objective planner as a facilitator to plan a family retreat instead of a free-for-all.

12. It ensures the examination of all the issues instead of a whitewash.

Bareither's dialogues are the best we have read in terms of integrating information and emotional issues. His query delves not just into technical information but how the family typically communicates, concerns of each member, views and feelings around succession, and their personal vision of future involvement.

MONEY IS AS MONEY DOES

A final legacy of money dialogue we would like to offer here was brought to us by David Davis, CFC, CLU, of Davis Financial Advisors in Chattanooga, Tennessee, which focuses on a big-picture conversation on the limited uses of money in our lives. There are really only four things you can do with money:

1. Earn it/Create it (forging excluded)
2. Save it/Invest it
3. Give it/Pass it on
4. Spend it/Use it

That's as far as it goes. Davis has found that by engaging in a dialogue with clients about the four uses of money, it helps people gain the proper perspective regarding the limitations and liberties of wealth. Nowhere is such a perspective more germane than as a preface to the estate dialogue. The legacy dialogue can be the most powerful dialogue of all. After all, in the long run, what is more important, the money we leave or the messages we leave with it?

EPILOGUE

"If people would come to me with real questions, something would come into being between them and me that does not exist now! The questioner is just as important as the answerer. A wise man is not a fountain of knowledge. On the contrary, he is helpless until someone brings him a question great enough to evoke a profound response."

Martin Buber

What is the greatest wealth we possess, that which has the potential to enrich our heirs for years to come? Is it not the magnificent singularity of our story—how we came to the place we are and became the people we are? Are the most enduring riches to be found in the memory bank?

Whatever wealth your clients have created, received, or inherited did not suddenly appear out of nothingness, out of a vacuum, and into being. No, there are stories behind every number on a spreadsheet—and those stories, not the numbers, represent the true wealth of who your clients are and who they hope to become.

They will trust this wealth to the party that best understands its origins.

Your clients wait, like an untapped gold mine of experiences, for someone to stumble upon a nugget in the flowing stream—a story, a lesson, or an event that reveals the vast richness they have within them. They wait for someone who understands their unique place in this world, their unique meanings and purposes, and who cares enough to ask and listen and understand their place in the whole scheme of things. They will continue to wait until someone asks an informed and thoughtful question.

Your clients are waiting for someone to draw out the best of who they are—their heroic moments through struggles, their meaningful relationships, and their aspirations for leaving behind something of significance in this world. The best that they are is found in their stories. You, the questioner, the biographer of your clients, has a unique opportunity with those who trust you to draw out the best in them and help them invest in it.

Once you have drawn their stories out, you have created a richer context for the work that you perform with their material assets. You have tasted the profound in fountains that others view as common. You are more than a financial advisor or planner when you ask important questions. You become an imperative figure in their unfolding story—a figure that brings to life and helps to animate the story within them by virtue of discovery and implementation.

When you begin your search for the transcendent and the significant in people's lives, you will not likely be drawn back into shallow waters. The first time a client thanks you by saying, "Thank you for asking that question," will be the beginning of a new agenda for fulfillment in your client relationships.

The questions you ask will define your place in your clients' lives. Great questions will redefine your place in this world. Fanatical curiosity is the DNA building block for your redefinition.

Abel, Alan. "Sweet Nothings—The Effects of Elderspeak." *Saturday Night.* October 1997.

Arnzen, Kris. "Values-Based Planning: Seeing the Whole Client, Part II." *Journal of Financial Planning.* April 1999. http://www.fpanet.org/journal/articles/1999_Issues/jfp0499-art12.cfm. Accessed 21 October 2004.

Bachrach, Bill. *Values-Based Selling.* Bachrach & Assoc. 1996.

Bareither, Karl. *Becoming a Wealth Transfer Specialist.* FBR Publishing. 2003.

Baumeister, Roy F., Jennifer D. Campbell, Joachim I. Krueger, and Kathleen D. Vohs. "Does High Self-Esteem Cause Better Performance, Interpersonal Success, Happiness, or Healthier Lifestyles?" *Psychological Science in the Public Interest.* May 2003. http://media.eurekalert.org/aaasnewsroom/2004/Baumeister-Self-Esteem-Paper.pdf. Accessed 5 November 2004.

Baumgarten, Elias. "Curiosity as a Moral Virtue." *International Journal of Applied Philosophy.* Fall 2001. http://www.umd.umich.edu/casl/hum/phil/curiosity.htm. Accessed 28 September 2004.

Bradley, Susan K. "Women Alone in Retirement." *Journal of Financial Planning.* September 2001. http://www.fpanet.org/journal/articles/2001_Issues/jfp0901-art4.cfm. Accessed 18 November 2004.

"Chapter 5: Effective Communication." University of Wisconsin Oshkosh College of Business Administration. http://mba.uwosh.edu/chap5.pdf. Accessed 27 September 2004.

"Characteristics of the Narcissist and Others with Personality Disorders." *Narcissistic Abuse.com.* 19 September 2004. http://www.narcissisticabuse.com/characteristics.html. Accessed 7 October 2004.

"Consumers Point to 'Must Haves' in the Ideal Shopping Experience in New Indiana University/KPMG Study." *About.com: Retail Industry.* 20 November 2000. http://retailindustry.about.com/library/bl/bl_kpmg1120.htm. Accessed 27 September 2004.

"Doing Well by Doing Good: Why a New Age of Philanthropy May Be Dawning." *The Economist.* 29 July 2004.

Donovan, Patricia. "Study Finds That Curiosity Is Key to Personal Growth in Many Spheres, Including Intimate Relationships." *UB News Service.* 16 December 2002. http://www.buffalo.edu/news/fast-execute.cgi/article-page.html?article=59960009. Accessed 29 September 2004.

Edelman, Susan. "Curiosity and Exploration." Spring 1997. http://www.csun.edu/~vcpsy00h/students/explore.htm. Accessed 29 September 2004.

Edwards, Melinda. "How Are You, Auntie Elizabeth?" *U.S. Department of State: English Language Program.* 2003. http://exchanges.state.gov/education/engteaching/pragmatics/edwards2.htm. Accessed 18 October 2004.

Frankl, Victor. *The Doctor and the Soul.* Vintage Books. 1986.

"Fraud Tops Health Crises and Terrorism on Rankings of Seniors' Greatest Concerns, Finds Financial Freedom Study." *Financial Freedom Press Release.* 20 May 2004. http://www.financialfreedom.com/pressRelease/05202004.asp. Accessed 19 November 2004.

Frolik, Lawrence A. "Overview of Estate Planning Issues." Kid Source.com. http://www.kidsource.com/kidsource/content4/estate.dis.all.3.2.html. Accessed 2 December 2004.

Gabriel, Michelle. "Why Clients Leave." *Registered Rep.* 1 February 2001. http://registeredrep.com/mag/finance_why_clients_leave/. Accessed 1 December 2004

Gerber, Michael. *The E Myth.* HarperCollins Publishers. 1988.

Gladwell, Malcolm. *The Tipping Point.* Brown Little. 2000.

Grove, Hannah Shaw and Russ Alan Prince. "How U.S. Small Business Owners Find Their Advisors." *Financial Advisor Magazine.* September 2004. http://fa-mag.com/articles/sept_2004_pi.html. Accessed 19 November 2004.

Grove, Hannah Shaw and Russ Alan Prince. "The Concerns of America's Small Business Owners," *Financial Advisor Magazine.* July 2004. http://fa-mag.com/articles/july_2004_pi.html. Accessed 19 November 2004.

Horwitz, Michael B. "Reality Check." Financial-Planning.com. 1 May 2003. http://www.financial-planning.com/pubs/fp/20030501025.html. Accessed 30 November 2004.

"How Are You?" Culture Bridge: ESL Corner. 2004. http://www.culturebridge.com/esl/how_are_you.html. Accessed 18 October 2004.

Kashdan, Todd B., Paul Rose, and Frank D. Fincham. "Curiosity and Exploration: Facilitating Positive Subjective Experiences and Personal Growth Opportunities." Journal of Personality Assessment, *82*(3), 291–305, 2004. http://mason.gmu.edu/~tkashdan/kashdan.html. Accessed 18 October 2004.

Lincoln Long Life[SM] Institute. "More Seniors Turn to Financial Advisors during Retirement." *Journal of Financial Planning.* 11 November 2004. http://www.fpanet.org/journal/BetweenTheIssues/Contributions/111504B.cfm. Accessed 16 November 2004.

Maki, Peggy. "Moving from Paperwork to Pedagogy: Channeling Intellectual Curiosity into a Commitment to Assessment." *American Association for Higher Learning Bulletin.* May 2000. http://

www.aahebulletin.com/public/archive/paperwork.asp. Accessed 1 October 2004.

Marcuss, Marnie. "Are Small Businesses Concerned with Credit?" Federal Reserve Bank of Boston. Fall 2004. http://www.bos.frb.org/commdev/c&b/2004/Fall/Credit.pdf. Accessed 20 November 2004.

Meyerson, Bruce. "Many Baby Boomers Creating Personalized Family Foundations." *Arizona Daily Star.* 5 April 2004. http://www.dailystar.com/dailystar/business/16716.php. Accessed 4 February 2005.

"Narcissism." *The Columbia Electronic Encyclopedia, 6th Edition.* 2004.

Nemy, Enid. "'Hello! How Are You?' (But Please Don't Tell Me. I Don't Really Want to Know)." *New York Times,* pg 34. 29 July 1990.

"Open and Closed Questions." Changing Minds.org. 2004. http://changingminds.org/techniques/questioning/open_closed_questions.htm. Accessed 18 October 2004.

Opiela, Nancy. "Estate Planning Peacemakers." *Journal of Financial Planning.* October 2003. http://www.fpanet.org/journal/articles/2003_Issues/jfp1003-art1.cfm. Accessed 23 November 2004.

"Pandora." 13 November 2002. http://www.colum.edu/centers/bpa/epicenter/pandora/themyth.html. Accessed 29 September 2004.

Parinello, Tony. "Tips for Keeping the Conversation Moving: When Dealing with Prospects, How Can You End the Silences and Boost the Selling?" Entrepreneur.com. 19 April 2004. http://www.entrepreneur.com/article/0,4621,315265,00.html. Accessed 20 October 2004.

Pecchioni, Loretta L. and Jon M. Croghan. "Young Adults' Stereotypes of Older Adults with Their Grandparents as the Targets." *Journal of Communication,* pgs. 715–730. December 2002.

Peninsula Community Foundation. "Center for Venture Philanthropy™ Unveils its Unique 5-Step Process of Successful Venture Philanthropy in New White Paper Report." 28 September 2004. http://www.pcf.org/about/cvp_whtpaper.html. Accessed 3 February 2005.

Perry, Bruce Duncan. "Curiosity: The Fuel of Development." *Scholastic.* 2001. http://teacher.scholastic.com/professional/bruceperry/curiosity.htm. Accessed 27 September 2004.

"Positive Moods and Emotions: Curiosity." eHappyLife, LLC. 4 April 2004. http://www.ehappylife.com/custom/pollresult91.html. Accessed 1 October 2004.

Pullen, Courtney. "A Relationship of Shared Experience." *Journal of Financial Planning.* February 2001. http://www.fpanet.org/journal/articles/2001_Issues/jfp0201-art8.cfm. Accessed 21 October 2004.

Scanlon, Chip. "Tools of the Trade: The Question: Reporters Ask Too Many Questions That Suppress, Rather Than Produce, Information." *PoynterOnline.* 23 October 2001. http://www.poynter.org/content/content_view.asp?id=5075. Accessed 19 October 2004.

Society for the Advancement of Education. "Brain Development Is Remarkable During First Few Years—Research Results and Child Management Advice." *USA TODAY.* August 1999.

Stephens, John. "The Story of Client X." Financial-Planning.com. 1 April 2003. http://www.financial-planning.com/pubs/fp/20030401016.html. Accessed 3 December 2004.

"Survey Shows Optimism among Small Businesses Despite Economic Concerns." Intuit press release. 20 December 2002. http:/

/www.intuit.com/about_intuit/press_releases/2002/12-20 .html. Accessed 18 November 2004.

"Synopsis of John Miller's *Egotopia: Narcissism and the New American Landscape.*" Amazon.com. 2003. Accessed 7 October 2004.

Taflinger, Richard F. "Curiosity Killed the Cat: Curiosity and Advertising." 27 May 1996. http://www.wsu.edu:8080/~taflinge/curious.html. Accessed 27 September 2004.

Tanner, Lisa. "Small Businesses Are Adapting to the Slow Economy and Developing Strategies to Succeed." Business Training Library. 15 November 2002. http://www.bizlibrary.com/news_smallfirms.asp. Accessed 18 November 2004.

"The Advisor-Client Relationship." HNW, Inc. 2003. http://www.hnw.com/intelligence/market-advisorclient.jsp. Accessed 1 December 2004.

Williams, Angie and Jon F. Nussbaum. *Intergenerational Communication across the Life Span.* Mahwah, New Jersey: Lawrence Erlbaum Associates, Inc. 2001.

Williams, Angie and Virpi Ylänne-McEwen. "Elderly Lifestyles in the 21st Centruy: 'Doris and Sid's Excellent Adventure.'" *Journal of Communication,* pgs. 4–8. September 2000.

On the following pages are samples of Life Transitions and Life Goals discovery research developed by the Financial Life Planning Institute (http://wwwflpinc.com). These samples offer the following information for each life concern or goal:

- Overview
- General Considerations
- Discovery Questions
- Financial Implications
- Educational Resources

You will notice a difference between the discovery questions for life transitions and life goals. The questions for the life transitions are highly idiosyncratic because each transition has broad implications for each individual's lifestyle and future. In the discovery questions for the life goals, it was necessary to follow a pattern applicable to all goals, including: "What obstacles do you see that could get in your way?" or, "How will you manage the obstacles?"

These discovery forms serve two purposes:

1. Preparing you for an informed conversation with your clients; and
2. Offering a framework for raising your clients' awareness of their concerns and goals. (Note: the "financial implications" and "educational resources" are helpful for raising your clients' awareness of how life changes can impact their financial situation.)

If you would like to incorporate this sort of discovery strategy into your practice, you can do so by becoming a member of the Financial Life Planning Institute (FLPinc.com). The Institute has researched and developed discovery materials for over 65 life transitions and over 55 life goals. This research is updated on a monthly basis. We believe that informed discovery is better discovery, and leads to more lasting solutions and relationships between advisor and client.

Begin an experimental career

Discovery Questions

1. Describe the experimental career you want to embark on. Include things such as hours, type of work, responsibilities, and location.

2. What really excites you about an experimental career and why is it important to you and your goals?

3. Do you have experience with an experimental career or trying a new job? Please explain.

4. Describe the time and financial commitment required to make your experimental career work. Do you feel you are prepared for this?

5. Who are the people that will be impacted the most by your experimental career?

6. What will you have to sacrifice in order to make your experimental career a success?

7. What challenges do you foresee in achieving this goal?

8. What preliminary steps do you need to take to make an experimental career work? Think of things you can begin today or a few weeks in the future.

9. Brainstorm and describe the ways in which an experimental career will change your life.

10. Consider your sense of motivation and desire, how certain are you that you want to begin an experimental career?

Create a parental pension

Discovery Questions

1. Describe the parental pension (income stream) that you would like to create for your parent(s), who this is for, and why you feel this is necessary.

2. Why is it important to you to be able to create this parental pension?

3. Have you created a parental pension before? If so, describe the experience.

4. How much time and money do you plan on committing to this parental pension?

5. How will the pension affect your parent(s') lives? Will it impact others?

6. You may need to sacrifice a few things to fulfill this goal. What might they be?

7. Describe the challenges that lie ahead. How can you plan for them and prepare yourself?

8. List the first five steps you plan to take to create such a pension.

9. How will your life change as a result of this pension and assisting your parent(s)?

10. Is this goal a realistic one for you at this time?

Create or fund a foundation

Discovery Questions

1. What type of foundation are you interested in?

2. What is the importance of this goal for you?

3. Can you think of any experiences in your past that can be related to this goal? Please explain.

4. How much time and money are you prepared to give towards this foundation?

5. Come up with a short list of people whose lives will be affected by your involvement with a foundation.

6. What are you prepared to sacrifice for this foundation?

7. Predict the challenges you may face as you strive to create or fund a foundation. Are there ways to avoid each of these challenges?

8. Are you aware of the steps you must take to either start a foundation or get involved with an existing one? Please explain.

9. What changes do you expect to see in your own life after fulfilling this goal?

10. Gauge your level of commitment to this goal and your certainty that you want to get involved.

Expand an existing business

Discovery Questions

1. Provide the specific details of this goal: (time frame, costs, figures, measurements, etc.)

2. What do you find to be the most important or exciting aspects of this life goal?

3. What sort of expansion projects have you undertaken before? Please explain.

4. How much money and time do you plan to commit to this project?

5. Whose lives will be impacted the greatest as a result of both pursuing and achieving this goal?

6. List the sacrifices you expect to make in order to make this expansion work.

7. Describe the challenges that lie ahead and ways to overcome them.

8. What steps are you taking or will you take to get started?

9. How do you expect your life to change during and after the expansion project?

10. Are you sure that this goal is right for you at this time? Please explain.

Go on an overseas mission trip

Discovery Questions

1. Please give some details on the mission trip you plan to go on. Where will you go? What will you do? Will you travel alone or with a group?

2. What excites you about an overseas mission trip? Why are you going?

3. Have you been abroad before? Was it for a similar program and/or goal? Reflect on any experiences that may be related to your current plans.

4. Estimate the amount of time and money you will be required to put towards your mission trip.

5. How will your work affect others? Think both on a large scale (internationally) and on a small scale (your own family).

6. What things will you need to sacrifice to go on such a trip?

7. There may be a number of challenges along the way. Are there any you can think of now? How could you overcome them?

8. What do you need to do to get started? List the first five steps you plan to take.

9. In what ways will this mission trip change your life?

10. Do you really want to commit to an overseas mission trip? Please explain.

Hire a coach (personal, career)

Discovery Questions

1. Looking ahead, in what ways do you expect your life to change as a result of working with a coach?

2. How certain are you that hiring a coach will help you and that you can remain committed to the program he/she develops?

3. What type of coach are you interested in hiring?

4. Why hire a coach? In what ways do you expect to benefit?

5. How much time and money are you planning on committing to this coaching program?

6. Have you ever worked with a coach before? If so, what was it like?

7. How will a coaching program impact the lives of those around you?

8. List a few of the sacrifices you expect to make to achieve this goal.

9. What are the biggest challenges you will have to overcome in order to hire this coach and how will you overcome them?

10. Outline the steps you need to take to begin your search for a coach and a program that works for you.

Live in another country

Discovery Questions

1. What country do you plan to live in? Describe the life you envision there.

2. Why is it important for you to live abroad?

3. Have you lived abroad before or made a large move? What do you remember about those experiences?

4. Estimate the amount of time and money you will need to commit to this goal.

5. Your decision to live abroad will impact the lives of others. Describe this impact in as much detail as possible.

6. What might you have to sacrifice to make the move?

7. Do you think that obstacles may occur when you plan to live abroad? Describe each one and ways to move beyond them.

8. There are a number or steps you need to take in order to move to another country. What things can you think of off the top of your head?

9. Living abroad will change your life drastically. What changes do you foresee in your situation?

10. Are you confident that moving out of the country is right for you?

Purchase a family vacation home

Discovery Questions

1. What type of vacation home do you and your family wish to purchase? Consider such things as location, type of structure, and your interests.

2. What will be the purpose of a vacation home for you and your family?

3. Have you ever purchased a vacation property before? What about a house? Reflect on these experiences.

4. How much time and money are you ready to commit to this project?

5. It is obvious that such a purchase will directly impact your family. Discuss this impact and include others who might be affected.

6. You may need to sacrifice a number of things to find and purchase a vacation home. What sacrifices do you think you may need to make? Are you prepared to make them?

7. Take a moment to think about the process of purchasing and managing such a home. What challenges might you face and how will you manage them?

8. Write down a few of the steps you may need to take in order to begin the process.

9. In what ways will purchasing a vacation home change your life?

10. How certain are you about such a purchase and your ability to handle it?

Purchase a recreation vehicle

Discovery Questions

1. Discuss the vehicle you plan to purchase and what you want to use it for.

2. Why is it important for you to buy it and what is most exciting about it?

3. Have you ever purchased a recreation vehicle before? If so, discuss the lessons you learned.

4. What time and financial assets are you prepared to commit towards this purchase?

5. How will your purchase affect the lives of those around you?

6. List the sacrifices you expect to make to fulfill this goal.

7. Reflect on the hurdles that may get in your way. How will you move beyond them?

8. Write the steps you will have to take in order to find and acquire the vehicle you want.

9. How do you think this purchase will affect your life? Think about changes in your personal, financial, and work life.

10. Are you sure that you want to see this goal to the end? Please explain.

Take a sabbatical or leave of absence

Discovery Questions

1. Sabbaticals and leaves of absence take many different forms and fulfill a variety of goals. Describe yours and what you want to achieve during it.

2. Why is it important for you to take a leave of absence? What excites you about such a venture?

3. Describe any experiences you may have with sabbaticals.

4. In terms of time and money, how much are you willing to commit to take a leave of absence and ensure that it is an enriching and rewarding experience?

5. Your decision to take a leave of absence will affect others. List these people and how their lives will be impacted.

6. What will you have to give up in order to take a sabbatical?

7. Can you think of any obstacles that may stand in your way? Describe the steps you can take to overcome them.

8. Create a list of the things you need to do in order to get started on a leave of absence.

9. How will your life change as a result of a sabbatical?

10. How certain are you that you actually want to commit yourself to a leave of absence?

Adopting a child

Introduction

For many Americans unable to have children, adoption is the perfect solution. Some choose to go through public agencies; others choose private organizations. Still others decide on welcoming an international child into their home. These forms of adoption are the most commonly known, however, the majority of adoptions in the US, a full 60%, are kinship adoptions in which an uncle, grandmother, or cousin agrees to adopt a child who has been orphaned or cannot be supported by his/her parents. All told, experts estimate that 1 million children have been adopted in the US. In fact, 60% of Americans have been touched by the adoption process in some way.

The adoption field is quickly diversifying as new types of adoption are developed, regulations on who is eligible to adopt change, and adoptions become a normal aspect of our society. As such, there are a number of options available for anyone contemplating this step. You may choose, like 10% of other adopting parents, to look abroad for a child in need of a family. Or you may decide to adopt a child of a different race in your own neighborhood. Transracial adoptions are growing and make up almost 8% of American adoptions. There are also a number of special needs children up for adoption across the country.

No matter which option you choose, it is important to familiarize yourself with the adoption procedure and its associated costs. These will vary with the type of adoption. For a public agency adoption the cost can be as low as a few dollars, while private or international adoptions can run up to $30,000. Knowing ahead of time the emotional and financial commitments required of you will help you decide if adoption is right for you and your family.

General Considerations

- Type of child you are looking for

- Preparing yourself for an adoption

- Finding a child to adopt

- Financial investment

- The home study

- Legal proceedings

- Welcoming the child into your home

- Teaching your child about adoption

Discovery Questions

1. Describe the adoption time frame you are working with.

2. What sort of adoption are you planning (international, agency, private)? How familiar are you with the process you have chosen?

3. Have you taken steps to prepare your family emotionally for the new child? Please explain.

4. In what ways have you or do you plan to prepare materially? This includes supplies you may have bought and remodeling or moving plans you may have made.

5. Do you plan to secure outside childcare for him/her? If so, please explain the details of this care and how much you expect to spend.

6. Have you taken time to consider financial issues such as a college fund, trusts, life insurance, and inheritance for your new child? If so, please explain.

7. How will your career be affected by a new child?

8. List the top five issues you want to address at this point related to the adoption.

Financial Considerations

- Costs related to adopting a child
- Cash flow considerations regarding adopting a child
- Asset management issues in regards to adopting a child
- Debt management considerations associated with adopting a child
- Risk management (insurance) considerations related to adopting a child
- Tax planning considerations related to adopting a child
- Estate or legacy issues related to adopting a child

Educational Resources

1. Real Parents, Real Children: Parenting the Adopted Child
- by Holly Van Gulden and Lisa M. Bartels-Rabb

A useful guide for raising your adopted son or daughter. Includes topics such as discussing adoption with your child and overcoming obstacles only adoptive families face.

2. Raising Adopted Children: Practical Reassuring Advice for Every Adoptive Parent
- by Lois Ruskai Melina

This books gives thoughtful advice on raising an adopted child based on insights from psychologists and doctors, as well as parents who have raised their own adopted children.

3. Adoption.org

This site features a variety of articles for parents looking to adopt and for others involved in the process. Articles discuss issues such as talking to your child about their own adoption and how to prepare your family for the new arrival.

http://www.adoption.org

4. American Adoptions.com

An informative site run by a private agency with information on how to begin the process and personal stories from other families who have gone through the process before.

http://www.americanadoptions.com

5. Nolo.com

A legal site providing answers to frequently asked questions. Under the heading "Caring for Children" this site covers such topics as legal procedures, agencies, and home visits related to adoption.

http://www.nolo.com

Child preparing for college

Introduction

The college brochures are beginning to pour in. The guidance office is sending home announcements about the SAT and ACT. Coaches from universities across the nation begin showing up at practices and games. The signs are all there: it's time to think seriously about college for your child.

High school students have a number of options. Some will choose to enter the work force immediately, while others will decide to take a year off. Still other graduates will choose to go on to higher education. In fact, according to the National Center for Educational Statistics, over 60 percent of high school seniors go on to some sort of postsecondary education.

For both students and parents, the admissions process and navigating the first year of college can be confusing and difficult. There are a number of deadlines to meet, tests to take, and forms to fill out. At the same time, you and your child will visit a variety of schools across the country to find just the right one. You will also need to make certain financial decisions as you plan for the high cost of tuition and room and board. Studies show that the average four-year school charges approximately $14,000 a year and almost 55 percent of students receive some sort of financial aid. For many, the process of wading through financial aid, loans, and scholarships is both difficult and time consuming. The average family spends 25 to 50 hours filling out forms, researching options, and selecting the best financial aid options. It may seem impossible at this point, but it's important to remember that starting early is the key. Give yourself time to cover each step as well as look through the incredible number of resources available. If 15 million other families can do it, so can yours.

General Considerations

- Your child's skills and goals

- Researching schools

- Visiting potential schools

- School's location

- School's living conditions

- Standardized tests

- Applications

- Recommendations

- Scholarships

Discovery Questions

1. How much thought have you and your child given to post-secondary education? What are your child's college plans?

2. Please list the steps you have taken to help him/her prepare.

3. What concerns do you still have about the process?

4. Do any of your children attend private school or receive private tutoring to help prepare for college? If yes, please describe and estimate the annual expense.

5. What sort of interests do your children have such as art, music, drama, horseback riding, sports, etc.? Have they committed to ongoing lessons or specialized training? If so, describe this training and the annual cost. How long do you expect to continue paying for such education/training?

6. Estimate the cost of college applications and standardized tests for your child as he/she prepares for college.

7. How will the expenses for education/training and the application process affect your family budget?

8. List the resources you plan to draw on or are currently using to pay for these expenses. Include any sources of financial assistance, savings, loans, or liquidation of assets.

9. Can your child help cover the cost with an after-school or summer job? Have you discussed this option with your child?

Financial Considerations

- Costs associated with your child preparing for college
- Cash flow considerations regarding your child preparing for college
- Asset management issues regarding your child preparing for college
- Debt management considerations concerning your child preparing for college
- Risk management (insurance) issues regarding your child preparing for college
- Tax planning considerations related to your child preparing for college
- Estate or legacy considerations regarding your child preparing for college

Educational Resources

1. FinancialAid.com

As an education finance leader, FinancialAid.com is committed to helping students and their parents get the money they need for college. Above all, we're committed to providing you with the best customer service in the business, with highly trained loan counselors to guide you through every step of the way.

http://www.financialaid.com

2. Free Money for College: A Guide to More Than l,000 Grants and Scholarships for Undergraduate Study
by Laurie Blum

A guide that covers the major scholarships and loans available to undergraduate students. Each scholarship is listed with contact information, eligibility requirements, and deadlines. Includes tips for applying for scholarships and how to find additional sources of aid.

3. Ed.gov

An essential site to help you and your child prepare for college and the application procedure.

http://www.ed.gov/pubs/Prepare/index.html

4. U.S. Department of Education

The U.S. Department of Education's website with information on government loans and filling out FAFSA forms.

http://www.fafsa.ed.gov

5. College Scholarships.com

An important resource which provides links to scholarship searches on the Internet.

http://www.college-scholarships.com/free_scholarship_searches.html

Develop or review an estate plan

Introduction

"My life is too busy to tackle estate planning."

"I don't have to plan for my family, I have life insurance."

"I'm simply focused on paying my bills now. Worry about the future? I'll do it later."

"I don't want to think about death, I've just barely started living!"

Whether from laziness, denial, ignorance, or sheer lack of time, thousands of Americans put off developing an estate plan. In fact, a study by Rutgers University shows that nearly 70 percent of Americans die without a will! This leaves many families unprotected and unable to direct the financial outcome of a loved one's death.

If you care about your family and their future it is vitally important to begin developing an estate plan today. Doing so can protect your assets from heavy taxation, provide more for your family after you are gone, and establish guardians for those you love.
Once you have written a will and planned your estate, don't think that it is set in stone. As your life changes and your financial situation evolves, your will should grow with you. Make estate planning and review of your will a normal part of your routine. Doing so will keep your legal documents up to date and provide the best form of protection and support for your family.

General Considerations

- Wealth protection
- Wills
- Testamentary trust
- Living trusts
- Probate
- Executor
- Financial and legal advisors
- Taxes
- State laws

Discovery Questions

1. When was the last time your estate plan was reviewed and/or updated? Did this result in any significant modifications to your estate plan? Please explain.

2. What is it that you would most like to protect and preserve in your life for the people and causes that are important to you?

3. Have you reviewed all of the important estate planning tools such as trusts with your estate planning advisor or attorney?

4. What real estate, physical assets (automobiles, household items, etc.), and financial property (securities, loans receivable, insurance policies, etc.) need to be addressed in your estate plan? List all assets and current value.

5. Are there charitable or gift funds, scholarships, etc. that you would like to set up as a part of your estate plan? Explain.

6. Following your death, will your beneficiaries require financial advice regarding the management and/or liquidation of assets? Explain.

7. As part of your estate plan, do you have Advanced Directives including Power of Attorney, Durable Power of Attorney for Health Care, and a Living Will? Please explain.

Financial Considerations

- Costs associated with developing or reviewing your estate plan
- Cash flow considerations related to developing or reviewing your estate plan
- Asset management issues in regards to developing or reviewing your estate plan
- Debt management considerations involved in developing or reviewing your estate plan
- Risk management (insurance) considerations in regards to developing or reviewing your estate plan
- Tax planning considerations in regards to developing or reviewing your estate plan
- Estate or legacy issues related to developing or reviewing your estate plan

Educational Resources

1. The American Bar Association Guide to Wills and Estates: Everything You Need to Know About Wills, Trusts, Estates, and Taxes
- by American Bar Association Staff

A comprehensive legal source that answers most questions related to wills, state laws, trusts, taxes, healthcare directives, and other concerns.

2. Beyond the Grave: The Right Way and the Wrong Way of Leaving Money to Your Children and Others
- by Gerald M. Condon and Jeffrey L. Condon

This book offers interesting and thought provoking advice on how to create an estate plan that minimizes the conflict and stress your family may go through after your death.

3. Your Living Trust and Estate Plan: How to Maximize Your Family's Assets and Protect Your Loved Ones
- by Harvey J. Platt and Don Kracke

This is a helpful guide with information on living trusts and other areas of estate planning. Included is an informative glossary of legal and financial terms related to estate planning.

4. National Association of Financial & Estate Planning

A great overview of what to expect in estate planning and the different options available to you as you develop a plan.

http://www.nafep.com/estate_planning

5. EstatePlanningLinks.com

This site offers an extensive list of links to other pages that should be consulted in reviewing and developing any estate plan.

http://www.estateplanninglinks.com

Going through a divorce or separation

Introduction

Experts estimate that the likelihood of a new marriage ending in divorce is over 40%. As such, separations and divorces have become an important and central life transition for many Americans in the past few decades. To deal with this life changing issue as well as the difficulties that may result, it is important to understand the process and how it might affect your life.

Divorces and separations stem from a number of causes. Researchers list issues such as incompatibility, abuse, lack of emotional support, and sexual problems. Financial issues also contribute as almost 70% of married couples argue over money. Look at your own situation to determine what the contributing factors are and whether mediation will help.

No matter what the causes of your divorce may be, you will definitely feel the costs and effects of this separation. Without your spouse, you may become solely responsible for your own support. For women in particular this is a difficult part of the transition. The U.S. Census reports that after a divorce, the average woman experiences a 45% drop in her standard of living. For both genders, the actual cost of a divorce in time and money is also a consideration. The average divorce costs $20,000 and lasts about one year. In addition, there may be children to think about; statistics show that 1 million children are affected by new divorces every year. Whatever you situation may be, experts and experienced couples agree that it's vital for you to seriously consider the financial implications of this transition as well as prepare for the entire process.

General Considerations

- Seeking help

- Children

- Religious beliefs and morals

- Emotionally prepared to be alone

- Financial stability

- Division of assets

- Legal proceedings

- Hiring an attorney

Discovery Questions

1. What is/are the main reason(s) why you are currently involved in a divorce or separation?

2. How far are you along in your divorce or separation and how would you describe your progress up to this point?

3. What has been your biggest challenge(s) up to this point? How about upcoming challenges? Please explain.

4. Are there children involved and, if so, what are your desires regarding physical and legal custody?

5. Will you likely be giving or receiving child support or alimony? Please explain.

6. How have the family finances been managed before your divorce or separation? Please describe your role.

7. What are some of the more important financial responsibilities you will have to accept after your divorce or separation?

8. What is your understanding of how your divorce or separation will affect your employer sponsored retirement plan and/or pension plan?

9. What, if any, insurance coverage will you lose as a result of this divorce or separation?

10. Overall, how do you expect your life to change after your divorce or separation?

Financial Considerations

- Costs associated with your divorce or separation
- Cash flow considerations regarding your divorce or separation
- Asset management considerations regarding your divorce or separation
- Debt management considerations regarding your divorce or separation
- Risk management (insurance) considerations regarding your divorce or separation
- Tax planning considerations regarding your divorce or separation
- Estate or legacy planning considerations regarding your divorce or separation

Educational Resources

1. Divorce.com

Divorce.com is a site geared to spouses contemplating and seeking divorce. The site offers comprehensive coverage of topics and useful tools and links for the process.
http://www.divorce.com

2. NOLO.COM

This legal reference site discusses practical issues such as the difference between fault and no-fault divorce, child custody, and family court procedures. Written in everyday language, this site is easy to navigate and an important tool for anyone contemplating divorce.
http://www.nolo.com

3. Parenting Through Divorce

- by Karen J. Todd, M.C. and Nancy Barros

A helpful resource for couples with children. This book explains how children are affected by divorce and how they attempt to cope with the change. Additional topics include how to co-parent with your former spouse and how to keep children out of divorce disagreements.

4. The Smart Divorce: 200 Things You Must Know

- by Susan T. Goldstein and Valerie H. Colb

This guide offers advice from legal experts on preparing yourself for divorce and making the process as painless as possible.

5. Fighting For Your Marriage

- by Howard Markman, Scott Stanley, and Susan Blumberg

A highly publicized and very popular book that offers advice on saving your marriage. Based on extensive research and a highly respected plan, the authors teach readers how to discuss difficult issues and overcome relationship obstacles.

Phasing into retirement

Introduction

Not ready for a full out move into retirement? Don't worry, you aren't alone. Many people look forward to retirement but for one reason or another are not ready today. Maybe they aren't ready for the sudden lifestyle changes. Maybe it's lack of savings that's holding them back. Maybe they haven't reached the government's full retirement age. No matter what the reason, many people are choosing to phase into retirement instead of retiring full out.

Using this option provides a number of benefits. You can keep working and continue making payments to your retirement accounts and savings plans. At the same time you can begin enjoying some of the benefits of retirement. Cutting back hours and decreasing your work responsibilities at a slow pace can open time for personal activities, traveling, and family.

However, phasing into retirement is not something you should do on the spur of the moment or with little thought. Planning is of the utmost importance as you negotiate this transition. You will need to calculate your ultimate retirement date, optimize your savings plan, and create a phasing schedule with your employer. Make this life transition the beginning of a new and rewarding stage of your life.

General Considerations

- Talking to your employer

- Involving your family

- Handing over your work duties

- Cutting back work hours

- Checking over your financial situation

- Present lifestyle and needs

- Emotional preparation

- Look for new hobbies and interests

Discovery Questions

1. List the reasons you have chosen to phase into retirement.

2. As you phase into retirement, how long do you expect to keep working?

3. How will your job description change?

4. What effect on your income do you anticipate as a result of this transition?

5. Does your company currently have an official phased retirement program? If yes, describe your phased retirement options.

6. What benefits will your company provide during this period?

7. How will you invest the time made available via reduced or changed work schedule and responsibilities?

Financial Considerations

- Costs associated with phasing into your retirement
- Cash flow considerations related to phasing into your retirement
- Asset management issues in regards to phasing into your retirement
- Debt management considerations involved with phasing into your retirement
- Risk management (insurance) considerations in regards to phasing into your retirement
- Tax planning considerations in regards to phasing into your retirement
- Estate or legacy issues related to phasing into your retirement

Educational Resources

1. Seniors.gov

This is a great site for anyone beginning the transition into retirement with information on financial considerations, housing options, and medical issues.

http://www.seniors.gov

2. ADP.com My Paycheck

With outlines for retirement planning and calculators to help, this site offers practical advice on money and more.

http://www.adp.com/mypaycheck/features/retirement.html

3. Social Security Administration Online

Social Security, Medicaid, and other government programs for retired people can be complex and frustrating. Visit this site to get all the information you need to plan ahead and phase into your retirement.

http://www.ssa.gov/

4. The New Retirementality: Living Your Life And Living Your Dreams At Any Age You Want
by Mitch Anthony (Dearborn Trade, 2001).

Inspiring and practical, *The New Retirementality* illustrates how readers can achieve the direction and financial security necessary to live the lives they really want beginning now. Mitch challenges readers to abandon their traditional thinking about retirement by dispelling the seven great "retiremyths."

5. Retire on Less Than You Think: The New York Times Guide to Planning Your Financial Future
- by Fred Brock

A great planning guide for you and your family's financial stability after retirement.

Reconsidering investment philosophy

Introduction

At one point in your life you probably developed some sort of investment philosophy. Maybe it was when you got that first job, when you went away to college, or when your first child was born. However, time has passed and things have changed. The market has fluctuated and your needs may have shifted to new areas. It's time to go back to that plan and readjust.

"Readjust?! But I thought investments grew on their own and I could simply reap the benefits and wait to cash in." Investing is not a hand-off activity. Unless you count on being lucky all the time, you will have to periodically reevaluate your investment philosophy and the amount of risk you have taken on. Some people wait until major changes in their lives or in the market force them to take a look. However, you should check up on your plan periodically (one or twice a year). Those who take such proactive steps may see problems coming and can make adjustments. In addition, regularly reconsidering your philosophy helps your investments stay in synch with your life. Begin today by following a few easy steps and covering the bases below.

General Considerations

- Current lifestyle and new changes
- Evaluating current investments
- Investment goals
- Types of investments
- Market
- Risk
- Amount to invest
- Professional help and advice

Discovery Questions

1. How would you describe your current investment philosophy?

2. In what ways has your investment philosophy changed?

3. Can you think of any events or experiences that have influenced this change?

4. What adjustments do you feel will be necessary to better align your investment portfolio with your investment philosophy?

5. How do you plan on making the necessary adjustments to your investment portfolio?

6. List the steps you have already taken to make these adjustments.

7. Would you like assistance in choosing investments that align with your current investment philosophy?

Financial Considerations

- Costs associated with reconsidering your investment philosophy
- Cash flow considerations related to reconsidering your investment philosophy
- Asset management issues in regards to reconsidering your investment philosophy
- Debt management considerations involved with reconsidering your investment philosophy
- Risk management (insurance) considerations in regards to reconsidering your investment philosophy
- Tax planning considerations in regards to reconsidering your investment philosophy
- Estate or legacy issues related to reconsidering your investment philosophy

Educational Resources

1. The Intelligent Asset Allocator: How to Build Your Portfolio to Maximize Returns and Minimize Risk
- by William Bernstein and David M. Darst

This source offers a great overview of different investment options and how to increase your return while managing your risks.

2. Your Money Matters: 21 Tips for Achieving Financial Security in the 21st Century
- by Jonathan D. Pond

Pond's book discusses ways to secure your financial future and provides strategies for making wise and effective investments.

3. The Intelligent Investor
- by Benjamin Graham and Jason Zweig

This great guide features advice on how to invest wisely in today's market and make the changes necessary to ensure your success.

4. Fool.com
This financial Web site offers helpful and comprehensive advice on most investment issues.

http://www.fool.com

5. FinPlan.com
With helpful advice on drawing up an investment plan and strategies for making the most of your investments, this site is an important resource for reevaluating your investment philosophy.

http://www.finplan.com/invest/invmain.asp

Starting a new business

Introduction

The small business is the backbone of America. Though most people know the names of large corporations such as Nike, Microsoft, and General Motors, it is the small mom-and-pop stores on the neighborhood corner that keep the economy moving. In fact, recent business surveys show that 22.5 million independent enterprises exist in the US today. Of these, 16.4 million are sole proprietorships, 1.6 million partnerships, and 4.5 million corporations. The vast majority (a full 99 percent) are small businesses with less than 500 employees.

Realizing the importance of these, Congress created the Small Business Administration fifty years ago to provide helpful advice and financial assistance to small business owners. In the average year the SBA guarantees $10,000 million in loans to small businesses while SBA-backed small business investment companies bestow another $2,000 million. This money is put to good use as starting a small business is no cheap venture. According to statistics, the average sole proprietorship requires an investment of $6,000 to get off the group, while a partnership can often raise $20,000. It is because of this extra investment that partnerships have a higher rate of survival than do sole proprietorships.

This data highlights the importance of capital and money management to the successful small business. As you try to navigate this venture, keep in mind the importance of managing your financial resources. The first and best thing you can do is to begin securing the capital you need and to create a clear business plan. These steps will help you stay on course and hopefully make your business a success.

General Considerations

- Market
- Location
- Personnel and supply needs
- Funding
- Time commitment
- Legal procedures and paperwork
- Financial records and paperwork
- Taxes and insurance
- Your abilities

Discovery Questions

1. What type of business would you like to start?

2. How did you come to this decision?

3. What will be your role in the day-to-day operations of the business?

4. Have you developed a business plan and conducted market research? Explain.

5. Will your health withstand the demands of entrepreneurship?

6. Have you calculated your financial risks? Explain.

7. How long are you prepared to wait before making a profit?

8. Have you consulted with others who have had experience in the type of business you would like to own?

9. Are you able to obtain the capital necessary to start/purchase a business and keep it running while also avoiding cash-flow problems? If yes, what is your financing plan?

10. Have you chosen a legal structure for your business?

Financial Considerations

- Costs associated with starting a new business
- Cash flow considerations related to starting a new business
- Asset management issues in regards to starting a new business
- Debt management considerations involved in starting a new business
- Risk management (insurance) considerations in regards to starting a new business
- Tax planning considerations in regards to starting a new business
- Estate or legacy issues related to starting a new business

Educational Resources

1. American Bar Association Legal Guide for Small Business: Everything a Small-Business Person Must Know, from Start-up to Employment Laws to Financing and Selling a Business
- by American Bar Association and American Bar Association Staff

This guide is an useful resource for understanding your legal responsibilities and rights as a small business owner and employer.

2. Small Time Operator: How to Start Your Own Small Business, Keep Your Books, Pay Your Taxes, and Stay out of Trouble!
- by Bernard B. Kamoroff

This book is a comprehensive guide on starting and keeping your business in order. This guide also includes chapters on running an online business.

3. Nolo.com

This legal site offers valuable advice for business owners under its "Small Business" section. Topics include corporations, bookkeeping, and taxes.

http://www.nolo.com

4. Businesstown.com

This is a great site with links to resources on everything from hiring and firing to startup and selling.

http://www.businesstown.com

5. More Business.com

This site, created by other entrepreneurs, offers tips on starting a business, tools for keeping things in order, and examples of contracts and business plans.

http://www.morebusiness.com

A

AARP, 104
A/B List, 150, 152
Accountability-for-results
process, 161
Acumen Fund, The, 162
Administration on Aging, 105
Advertising, 52
Aging parent, 103–5
Alignment, 112
American Cancer Society, 165
American Medical Association,
52
Annual Survey of Client
Concerns, 107
Anthony, Tom, 169–78
Arnzen, Kris, 183
Association, 85–86
Atlantic Philanthropies, 159
Austin Social Venture Partners,
162
Autobiographical urge, 28,
39–40

B

Bachrach, Bill, 63
Background questions, 18–19
Bacon, Kevin, 14–15
Bareither, Karl, 190–91
*Becoming a Wealth Transfer
Specialist*, 190
Berman, Melissa, 158
Biographical inquiry, 32
Body language, 11
Bolder Options program, 164
Boundaries, 110–11

*Bridal Bargains: Secrets to
Throwing a Fantastic Wedding
on a Realistic Budget*, 123–24
Buffett, Warren, 116
Bureau of Economic Analysis,
173
Bush, George H.W., 131
Business Transitions Profile,
140, 141–42

C

Career tract, 20, 22
CareGuide.com, 105
CEI. *See* Curiosity Exploration
Inventories
Center for Venture
Philanthropy (CVP), 161
Child's Wedding Fund, 123–24
Cisco Systems Foundation, 162
Cleary Gull, 131–32
Client
    biography development,
    65–67
    boundaries, 110–11
    definition of wealth, 113,
    114–15
    discovery, 7
    expectations, 86–90, 90–91
    experience inquiry, 80–93
    financial experience, 82–86
    goals, 59–60, 116–28
    historical inquiry, 69–79
    interest in, 41–42, 46–49
    investment style, 109
    motivation, 12
    nature of money, 112–13
    principles inquiry, 107–15

    quality of life, 58
    resistance, 53
    satisfaction, 63–65, 91,
    178–79
    story, 57–58, 193–94
    transition inquiry, 94–106
    uniqueness, 27–28, 36–43
Clinton, Bill, 42–43, 131
Communication
    estate planning, 188–90
    expectations, 8, 90
    importance of, 178
    skills, 8–9
Community foundations,
158–59
Condon, Gerald M., 183–84
Connection points, 32
Connectivity
    degrees of separation and,
    14–23
    inquiries and, 18–23
    small world principle, 16–17
    specialization strategy and,
    15–16
Connectors, 16
Contentment, 77–79
Context, 61
Contextual information, 11–12
Controversial qualities, 4
Conversation
    beneficial, 47
    curiosity levels and, 2–4
    dominators of, 27
    empathetic behavior in, 11
    inquiry skills, 6
    intelligent inquiry, 25–26
    mistakes, 10–11
    monopolists, 5